Struggle In Paradise

STUART PERLMAN

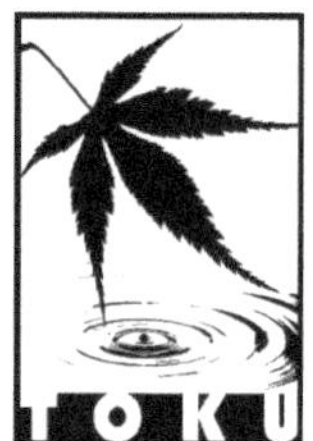

Copyright © 2018 – Stuart Perlman

Published by Toku Publishing, LLC

ISBN-10: 1-948820-26-9
ISBN-13: 978-1-948820-26-4

First Edition, July 2018

"Some people think we're just a bunch of lazy people out here - that's not true –we're just like anyone else who wants to live and make it – but it's difficult."

Jon, *Venice Beach regular*

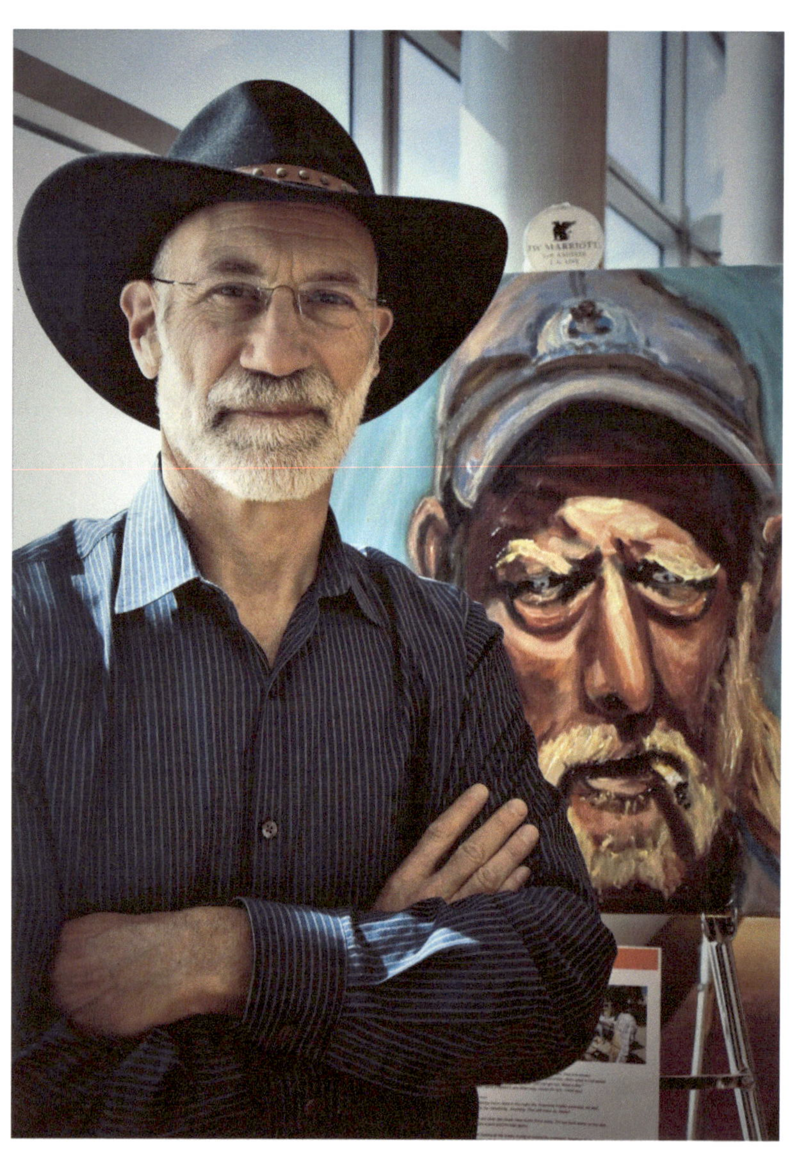

Forward

Homelessness is a complex issue that has been growing rapidly in Los Angeles and in many parts of the United States. It is a shame that in our great nation we have not been more proactive and effective in dealing with this tragedy. The fact is that many homeless people live in desperate squalor and die on the streets from assault, unsanitary conditions and untreated disease. The safety net in this country is sorely insufficient for those in trouble. But perhaps even more devastating is that these individuals are made to feel as though they are "nothing," that "no one cares" and that they are "alone, facing a reality that is unbearable." I want to shine a light on this reality.

My professional life has been "devoted to breaking the silence" and telling the truth about trauma and oppression and their powerful effects on people. In this book I aim to help individuals experiencing homelessness tell their "own truths through their portraits and stories. Almost every person I interviewed was a survivor of trauma before they became homeless, which contributed to their homelessness, and once they were on the streets they were repeatedly traumatized, making it even harder to escape. Through this project I hope to give a voice to this often forgotten and overlooked population. I also hope to expose the greatest truth of all: We are all people, we are all vulnerable, and each of us is just one thin, life-altering experience away from being homeless ourselves. Each day I work on this project I must remind myself, "there but for the grace of God go I."

Acknowledgements

I would like to acknowledge Wendy Levin, Ph.D. and Nancy Colman who have edited this book, curated my "Faces Of Homelessness" art exhibitions, and collaborated on our award-winning movie *Struggle in Paradise*, which documents this project. I would like to thank my wife Denise, my rock and soulmate, and my sons, David and Aaron, for helping me with this project. I would also like to thank Alex Cohen for his graphic design of this book and my publisher, Daniel Van of Toku Publishing. And many thanks to Vida Ahadian for her support and George Atwood, Ph.D. for his relentless encouragement.

This book is dedicated to those people experiencing homelessness who live and die on the streets every day in one of the wealthiest nations in the world.

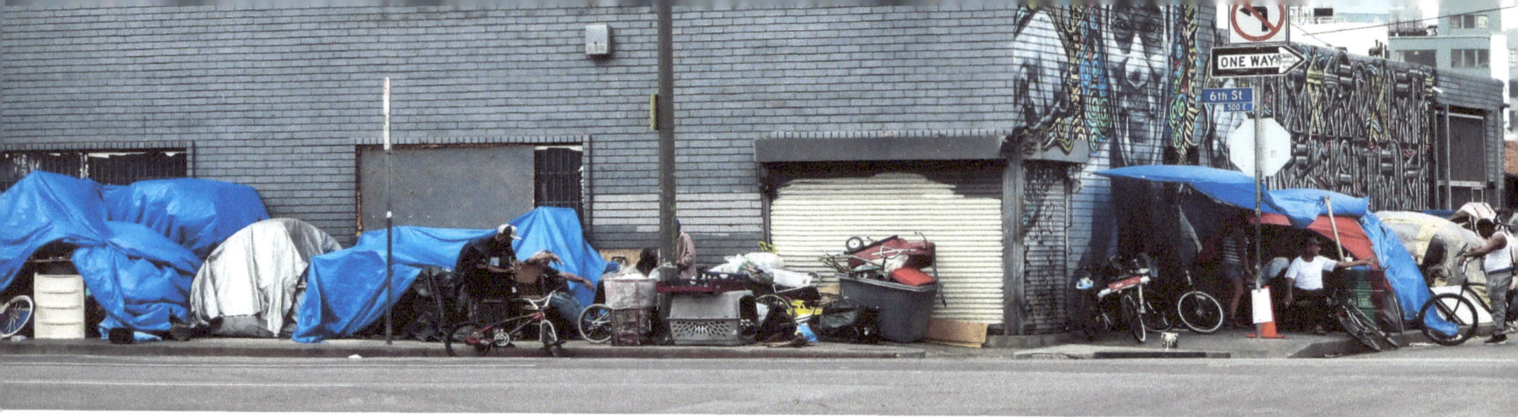

Introduction

I would like to share with you my own personal journey getting to know and helping those experiencing homelessness in the greater Los Angeles area.

I started painting 10 years ago, when my father died. His death was a wake-up call for me – a reminder of how fleeting life is and how I had better start doing more things I always wanted to that were truly meaningful and impactful. I was seeking a project with a powerful social message.

Nine years ago, I found it. I began painting portraits of the men and women I encountered living on and around Venice Beach. These were some of the most interesting people I had ever met – loving, kind, accomplished individuals who had experienced deep traumas and misfortunes. I listened to their stories and collected their artwork, poems and music. I painted the life experiences that were etched on their faces. Then, three years ago, I went down to Skid Row to paint individuals experiencing homelessness there as well. I now have over 200 portraits – each with a biography chronicling these life stories.

I believe that because I have been a psychologist and psychoanalyst for over 40 years, I have been able to gain the trust of my subjects and get their deeper truths. So many of these individuals' histories broke my heart. Many times, when I went home at night after painting, I felt like crying; I was overcome by feelings of guilt because I left behind people who had become dear friends of mine. They remained in their lives of desperation while I went back to my comfortable life. I can only hope that my time with them and the relationships we formed – along with the knowledge that their stories are being heard and shared – benefits them in some small way.

Project

The goal of this project is to put a face on the issue of homelessness. Formal portraits in oil on canvas are usually painted to immortalize the rich, famous and powerful. By painting formal portraits of my Venice Beach and Skid Row subjects, I am sending them, as well as others, a clear message that they are valuable human beings.

We usually try to avoid looking at people living on the street - to avoid seeing the pain and precariousness of life. I paint the faces of my subjects bigger than life, filling the entire canvas, so they cannot be ignored. By engaging with these portraits, one is looking into the eyes of these individuals, as they are looking into yours.

I have exhibited the portraits and biographies in this collection throughout Southern California and nationally for the past six years. This project is also documented in the film *Struggle in Paradise.*

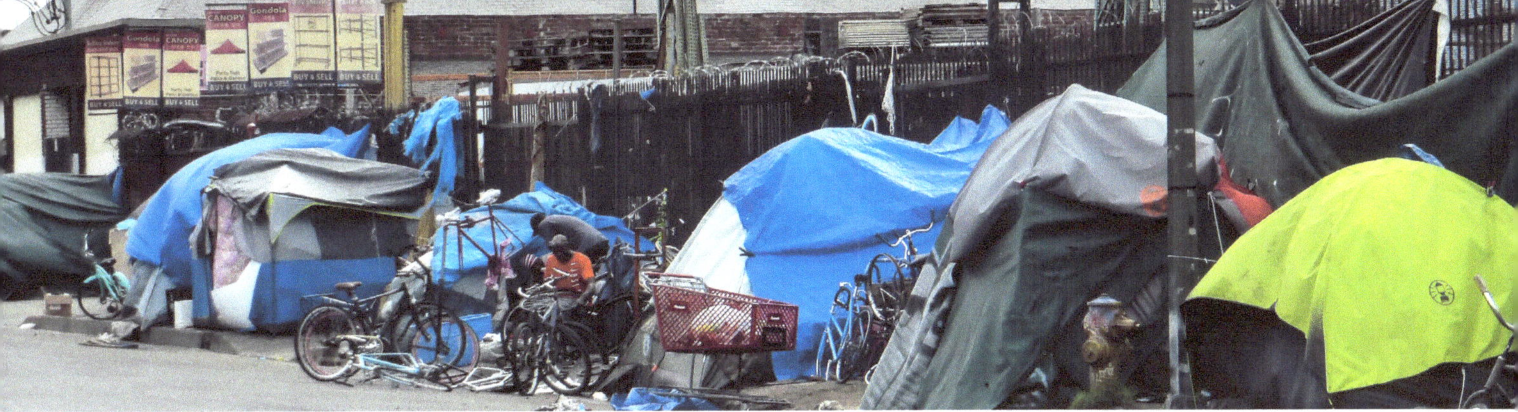

Impact

Most of my portrait subjects report feeling unseen and mistreated living on the streets. As I paint them I comment on what I think is admirable and heroic about them. Over time they usually become more talkative and smile. One person said he felt like he was a "ghost," but that my painting his "essence" for others to see made him "more present in this life." Others talked about feeling "worthwhile" being listened to and painted. Many bragged to friends about having their portrait painted, and some trumpeted that I was going to make them "famous" by sharing their art, poems and/or lyrics with others. Some said that I was doing "God's work," or that they "felt like Jesus for a day."

By the end of our sessions many of the people I paint seem to have more self-esteem. Some have been the "black sheep" of their families and considered failures; but now they are proud to send them a print of an oil portrait of them by a "famous artist."

Methodology

My painting methodology is simple. Before setting up my easel, I walk the same areas over several days, often repeatedly asking who is willing to be painted. Engaging homeless individuals to have their portraits painted and their stories told is a complex dance of gaining trust that can take months and at times, 25 to 30 different discussions over the years.

As I walk I usually give out money and food, and sometimes art supplies to people trying to make a living by creating art. I present myself as an artist whose goal is to illustrate that people experiencing homelessness are human beings just like everybody else; people who deserve to be seen and respected.

I avoid the more agitated or aggressive folks and anyone who I think is under the age of consent or unable to give consent. Everyone in the project must sign a release and is paid. If they agree, I bring my art supplies on a dolly and paint them within 10 feet of where they sit all day. I then spend many more hours at home finishing the paintings. For paintings on larger canvases, I instead take about 700 photos of the person and paint the entire portrait at home.

I leave each portrait unframed, to symbolize the four walls that are missing in these individuals' lives. Once completed, I photograph the paintings and make 8.5" x 11" prints. I then try to locate my subjects to give them the photos of their portraits. I have been mostly successful. Just about everyone is thrilled with the results, though some lament that I made them look too old or gave them "sad eyes." Many talk about who they will send the prints to and some ask for a second, third or fourth print. I give them envelopes and sometimes stamps.

Bill

I could not ignore the epidemic of people living on the streets even if I tried. Bill, 62, has waited for me most mornings just outside my office in West Los Angeles for 10 years now, because that is where he lives. Bill has become both a friend and a responsibility.

Bill starts talking to me about his pain and fears the moment he sees me. His childhood was a turbulent one. His father, a brilliant inventor and businessman, had great expectations for Bill, but he was violent and abusive when he did not believe those expectations had been met. Bill was a slow learner and his father berated him for this. Bill, perhaps as a way of maintaining his self-esteem, developed a style of fighting back. He was often angry and got into trouble.

At 17, Bill's parents signed him up for the military because he was under-age. He served in Vietnam for six years and was honorably discharged. However, Bill says that if he really "took in" what he had to do in Vietnam, he would be totally devastated.

After his father's death, Bill inherited his father's once- thriving business, which by that time was mired in debt due to his father's gambling. Unable to pay off creditors, Bill lost everything and became homeless.

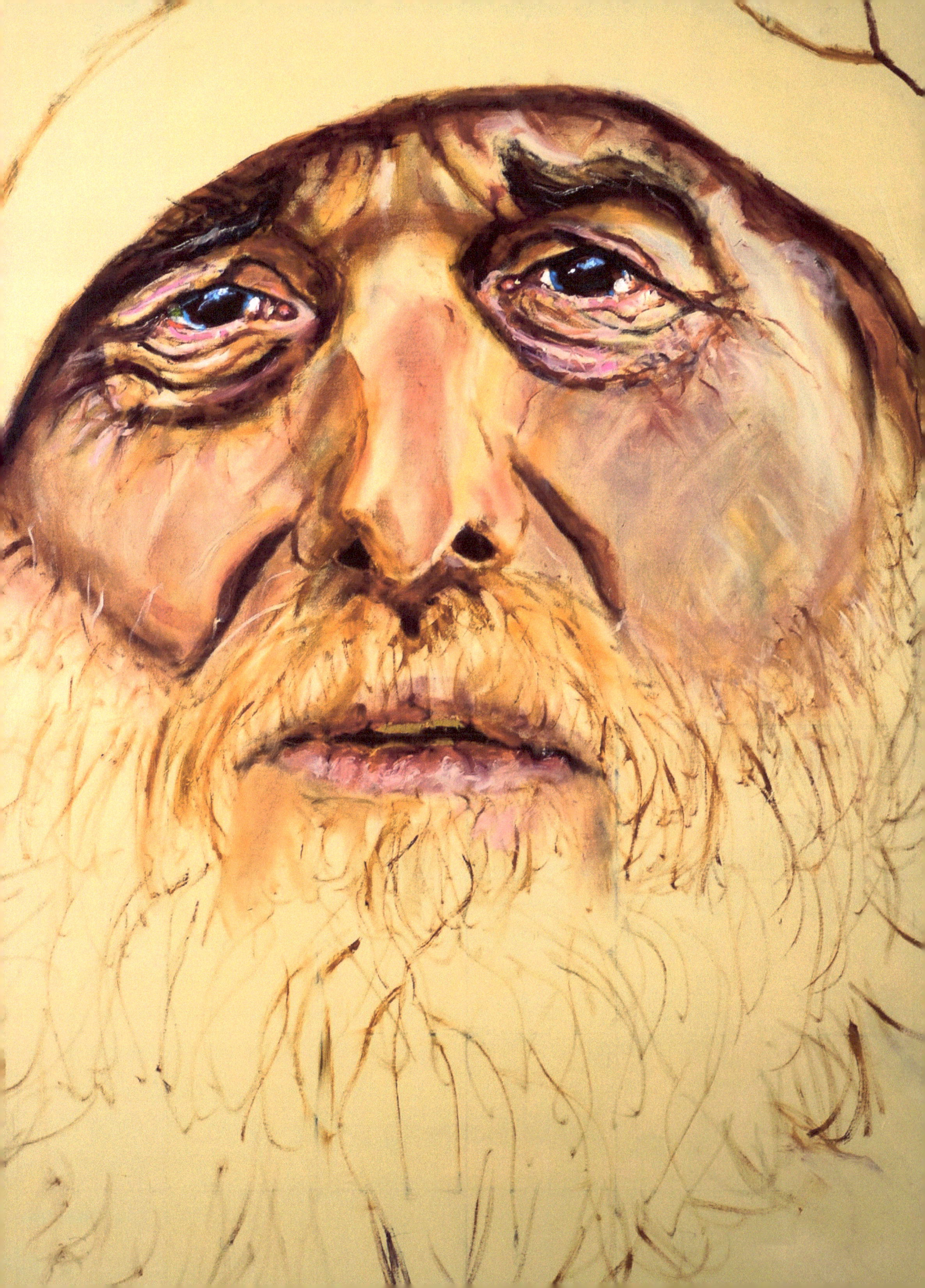

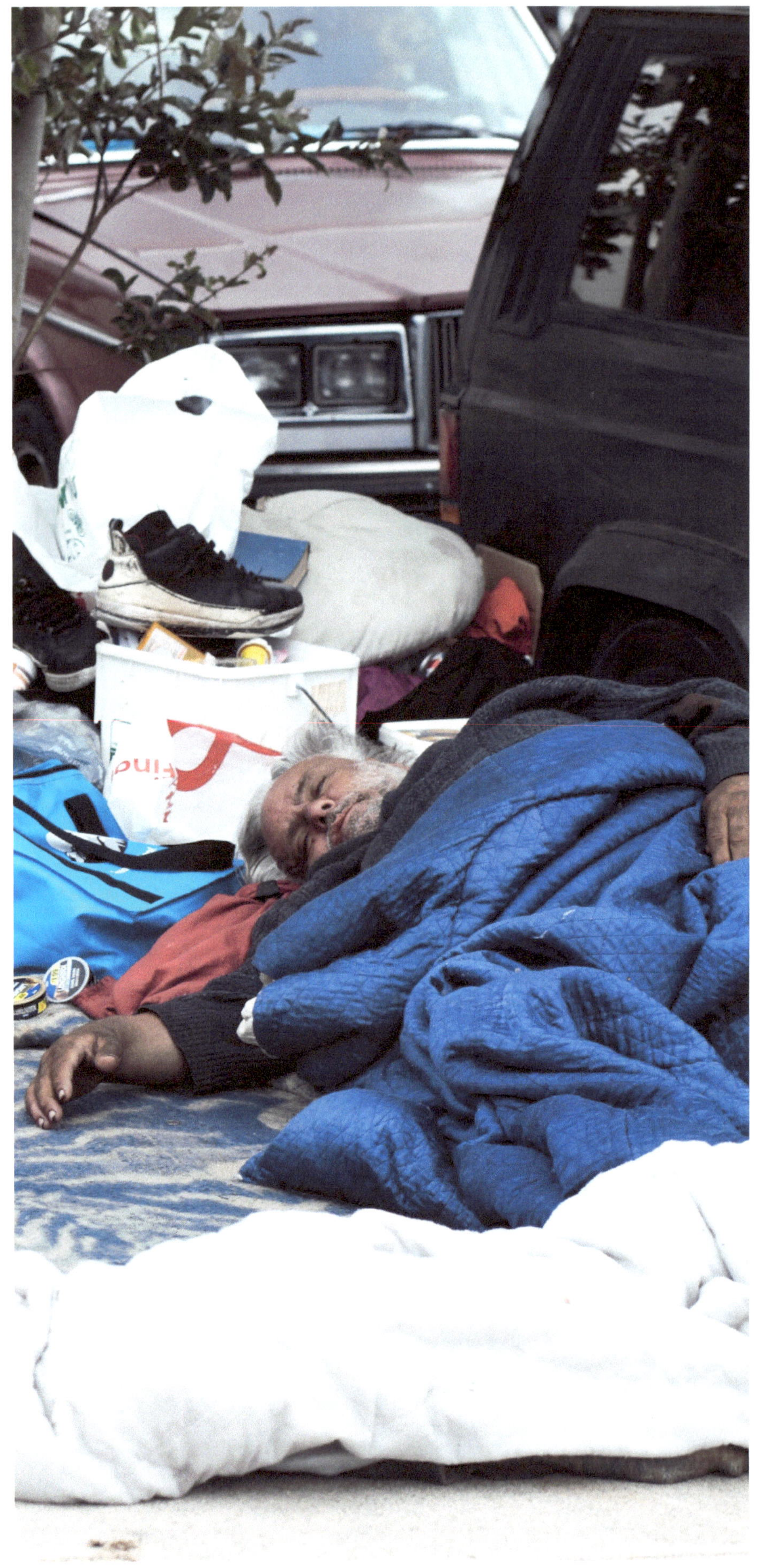

One reason I got involved in
helping and painting people
experiencing homelessness was
seeing this view of Roy outside my
office window for years.

Roy

Roy, 53, was a successful electrician in Arizona making a decent living when he learned that his mother was terminally ill. They had always been extremely close and so he relocated to Los Angeles to care for her. But life in L.A. turned out to be a nightmare that changed Roy's life forever.

First, he was hit by a car. The accident left him unable to walk. One leg is now completely useless and the other is severely impaired. Then, his beloved mother died. Roy was supposed to inherit her house and all her assets but was instead "swindled and evicted." Roy hired a lawyer, but he says that the system is impossibly slow and that is why he ended up on the streets.

Roy spends most of his time just lying on the sidewalk in West L.A. Occasionally "someone from an agency" comes by and gives him a bath and a haircut and then "returns" him to the sidewalk. Roy desperately wants to get his legs fixed and get back to work.

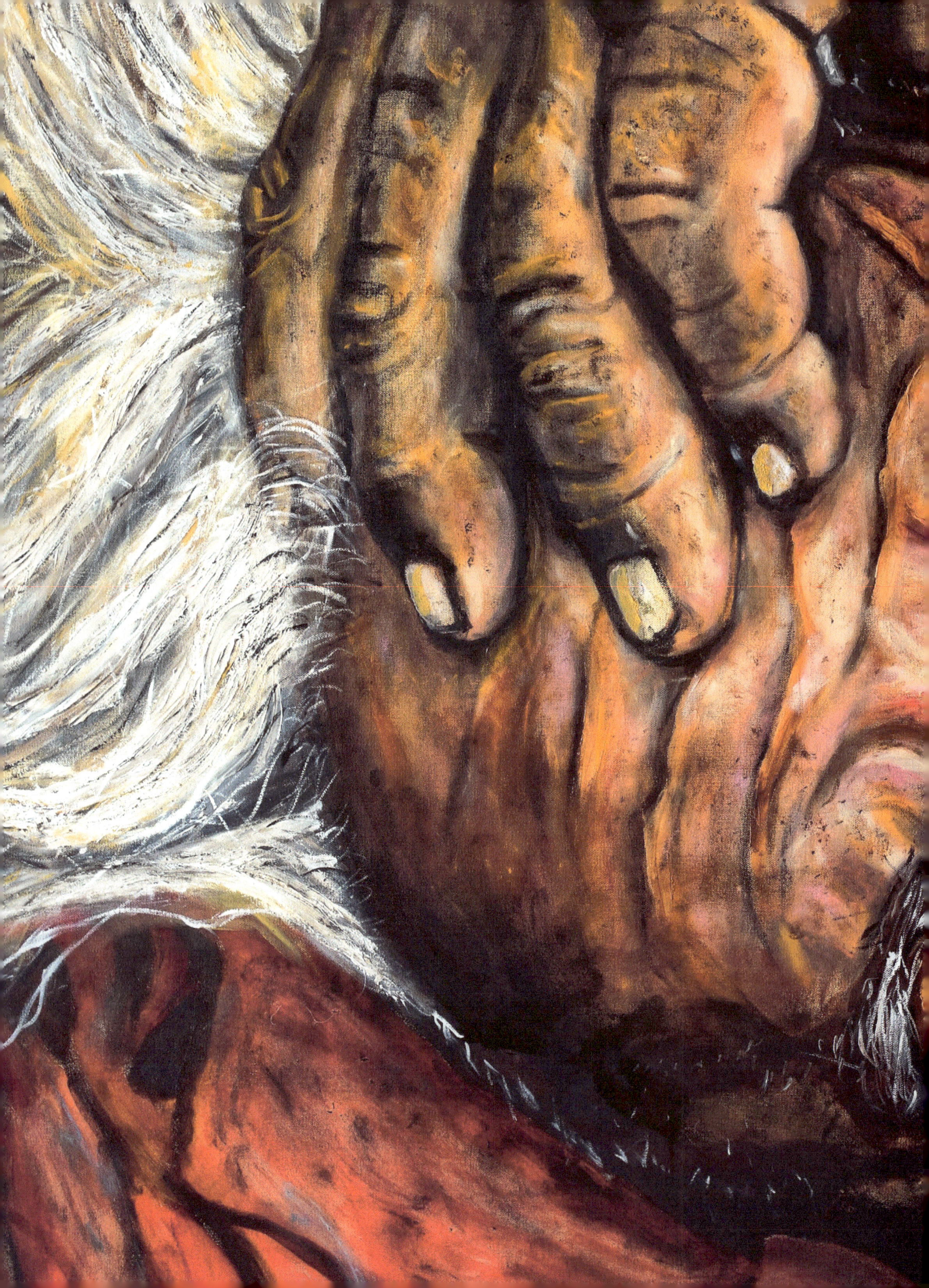

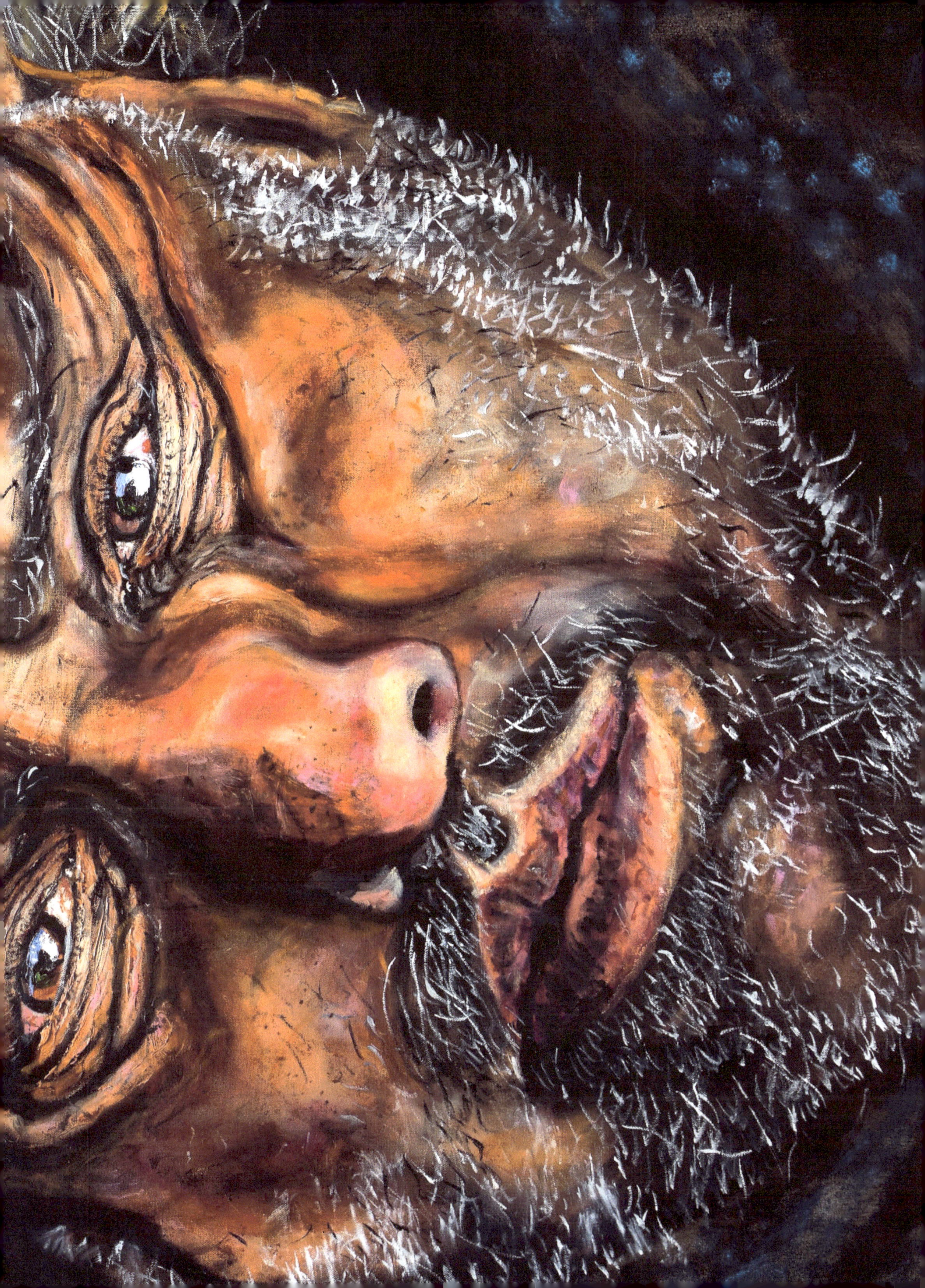

Smiley-Monkey

(☺ Monkey)

☺ Monkey, 18, was born in Redding, California, on a public transit bus. Her mom was a crack addict. ☺ Monkey has never lived at a permanent address or attended any school for longer than six months, however she recently got her GED.

☺ Monkey has been on the road since birth. Her mother was beautiful and a social butterfly. She and her mom made their living panhandling. Her mom had many boyfriends, most of whom were one-night stands. ☺ Monkey didn"t like any of them. She refused to talk to me about it, but she indicated that "bad things" happened. She said she has had a "crazy f***ing life." Her mother ultimately died from brain damage suffered after being hit by a truck, but the doctors said it was also all the drugs that killed her.

☺ Monkey met her dad for the first time just a week before I painted her; up until then she only knew that he was in and out of jail for being a "mean drunk and a drug addict." On their first meeting he hit her in the head and kicked her out of his house. She told me she will never speak to him again. Though her hopes for a relationship were dashed, ☺ Monkey says that somehow this encounter actually made her feel better because now a lot of things in her life "make more sense."

☺ Monkey tried to put a positive spin on these misfortunes by saying, "What doesn't kill you makes you stronger." But she looked so sad.

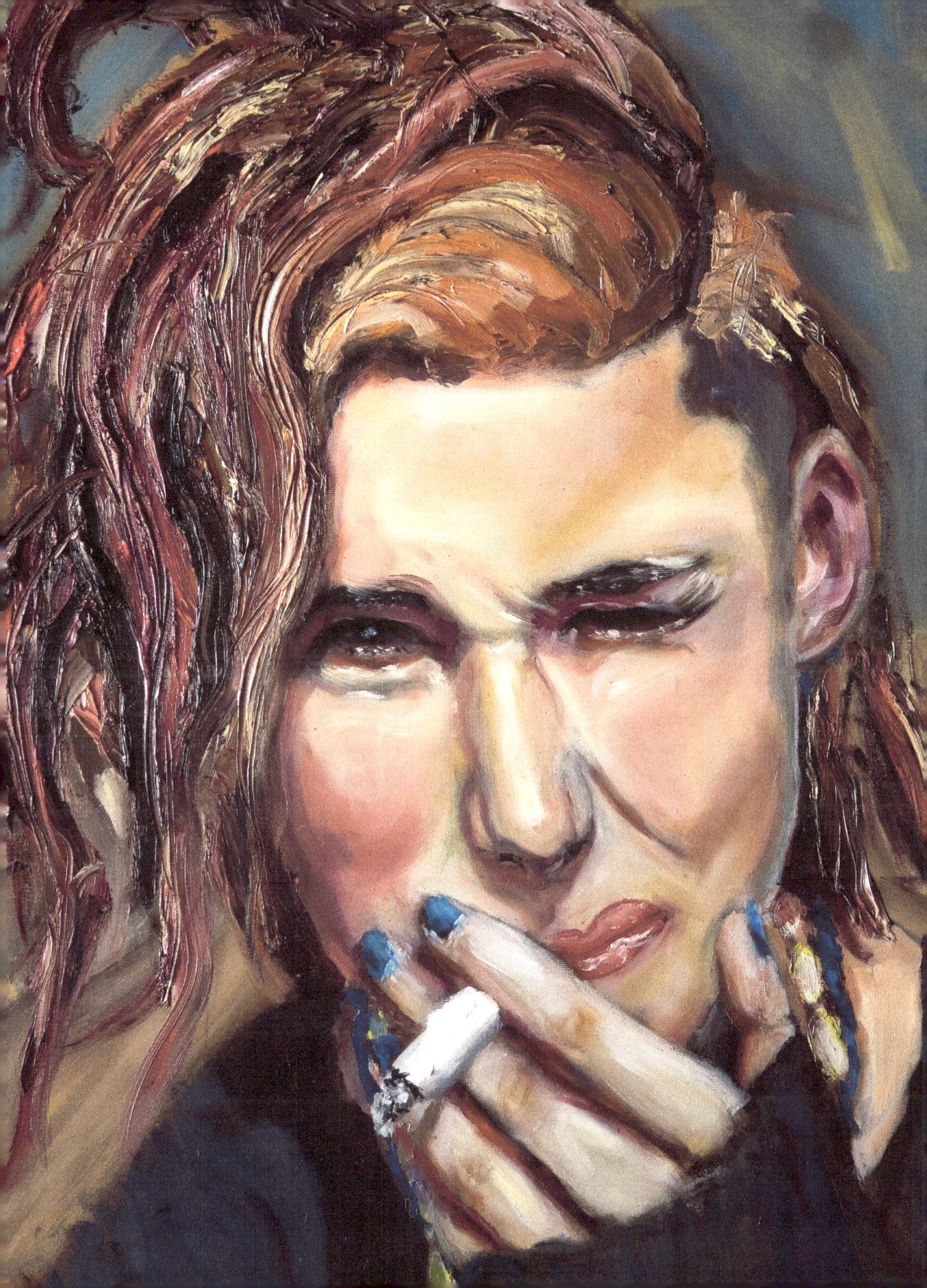

Dana

Dana, 43, was born in Glendale. She grew up in a stable home with her parents and a sister and led what she describes as a "good church life." But soon Dana began to hang out with the "wrong crowd" and got heavily involved with drugs – particularly crack cocaine. She had the first of her four children when she was just 16 years old. Her youngest, who lives with grandparents, is now 14.

Though she has tried to overcome her addiction, Dana has cycled in and out of treatment programs and continues to relapse. Dana admits that her family was once supportive, but she has let them down so many times she can no longer burden them. She now lives on the streets of Skid Row, cleaning houses, selling drugs and prostituting herself to get by.

In this portrait Dana is recalling her devastation over missing her youngest daughter's recent music recital. She wants desperately to get better but cannot figure out how.

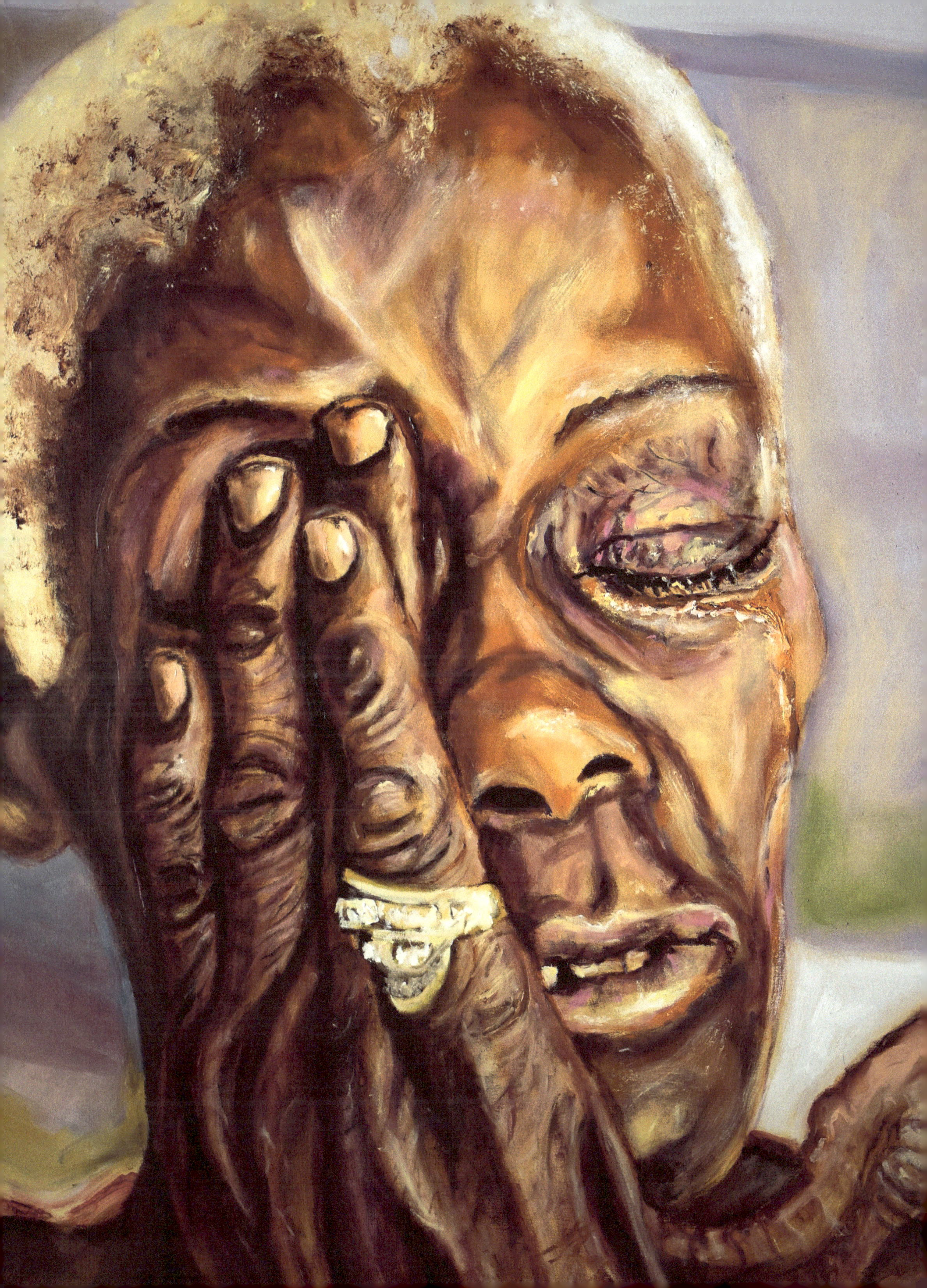

Patrick

Patrick, 28, is gorgeous, smart and quick-witted but there is something ghostlike about him. His maternal and paternal grandparents were immensely wealthy, but both his parents were drug addicts and served prison sentences. They were also irresponsible and negligent, and Patrick was physically and sexually abused. Despite being extremely intelligent, he always did poorly in school because he "didn't care."

Patrick got into drugs to "escape the pain" of his childhood. Ever since the age of 13 he has engaged in risky behavior, not seeming to care if he lives or dies. The best times in his life have been in juvenile detention or in jail because "somehow those environments made more sense" and allowed him to be surrounded by "some supportive people trying to help." Patrick graduated from State University of New York in electrical engineering and has had some jobs as an electrician, but they never lasted long.

Patrick was living on the streets in New York, but when "a drug deal went bad" he came to Los Angeles, where he is again homeless.

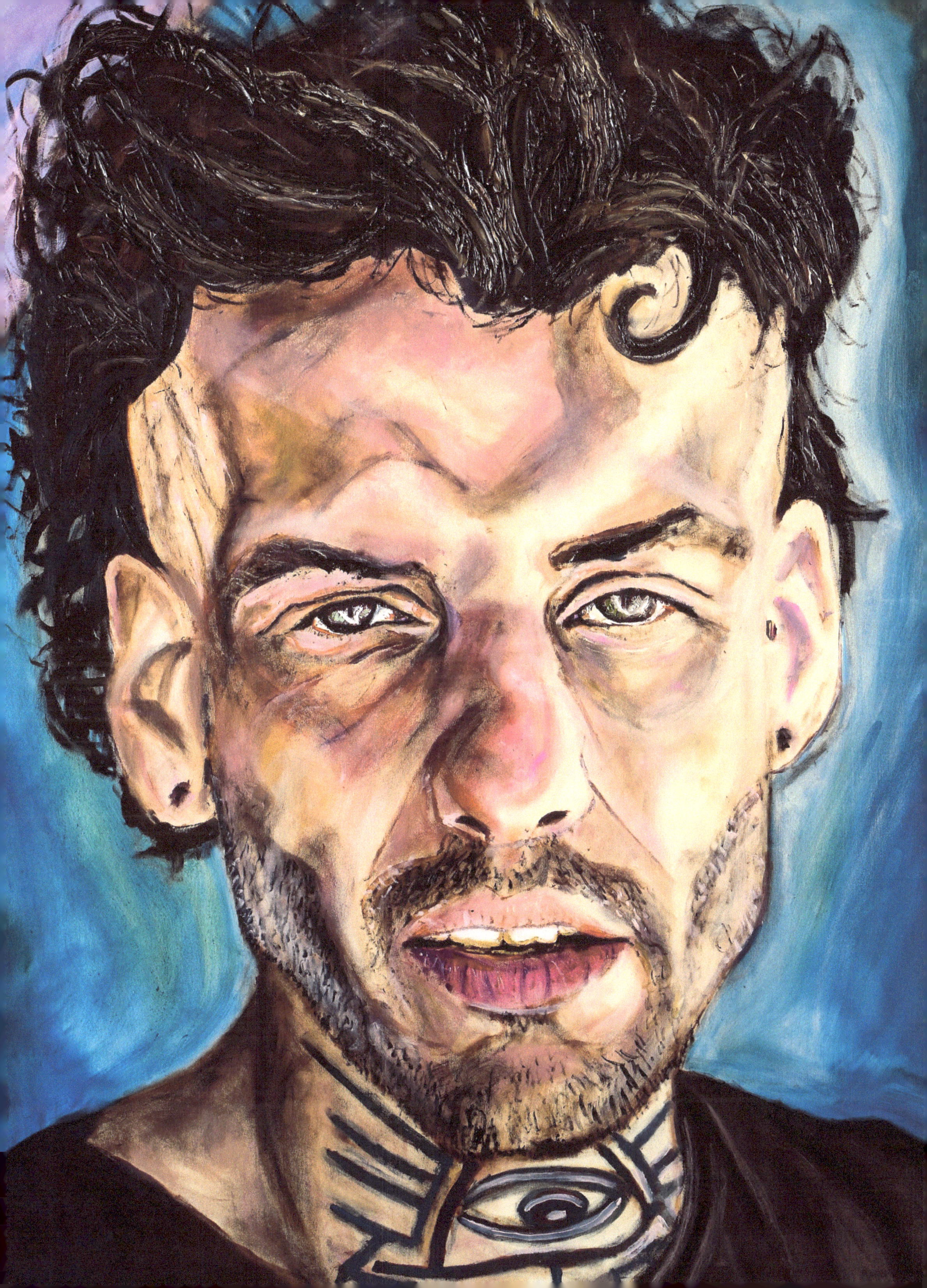

Corey

Corey, 20s, had an early childhood so terrible that he "cannot even talk about it." His father was "a raging drunk" and at the age of eight Corey's parents abandoned him in a parking lot. Somehow, he was found and delivered to his aunt and uncle, who raised him.

At 18, Corey enlisted in the Navy and became a Navy SEAL. As an expert marksman he did multiple tours in Iraq. But one mission led to his undoing: Corey was ordered to "take out a target." When Corey took aim at the target, the man held up an infant and put it between Corey's rifle and himself. Corey hesitated but his superior officer said, "Shoot the target through the baby!" Corey refused. He was court-martialed and dishonorably discharged.

Following this devastating series of events Corey had no place to go and became homeless on Venice Beach. His girlfriend Crystal (next in this book) is pregnant with his child. He desperately wants to get a job to support them.

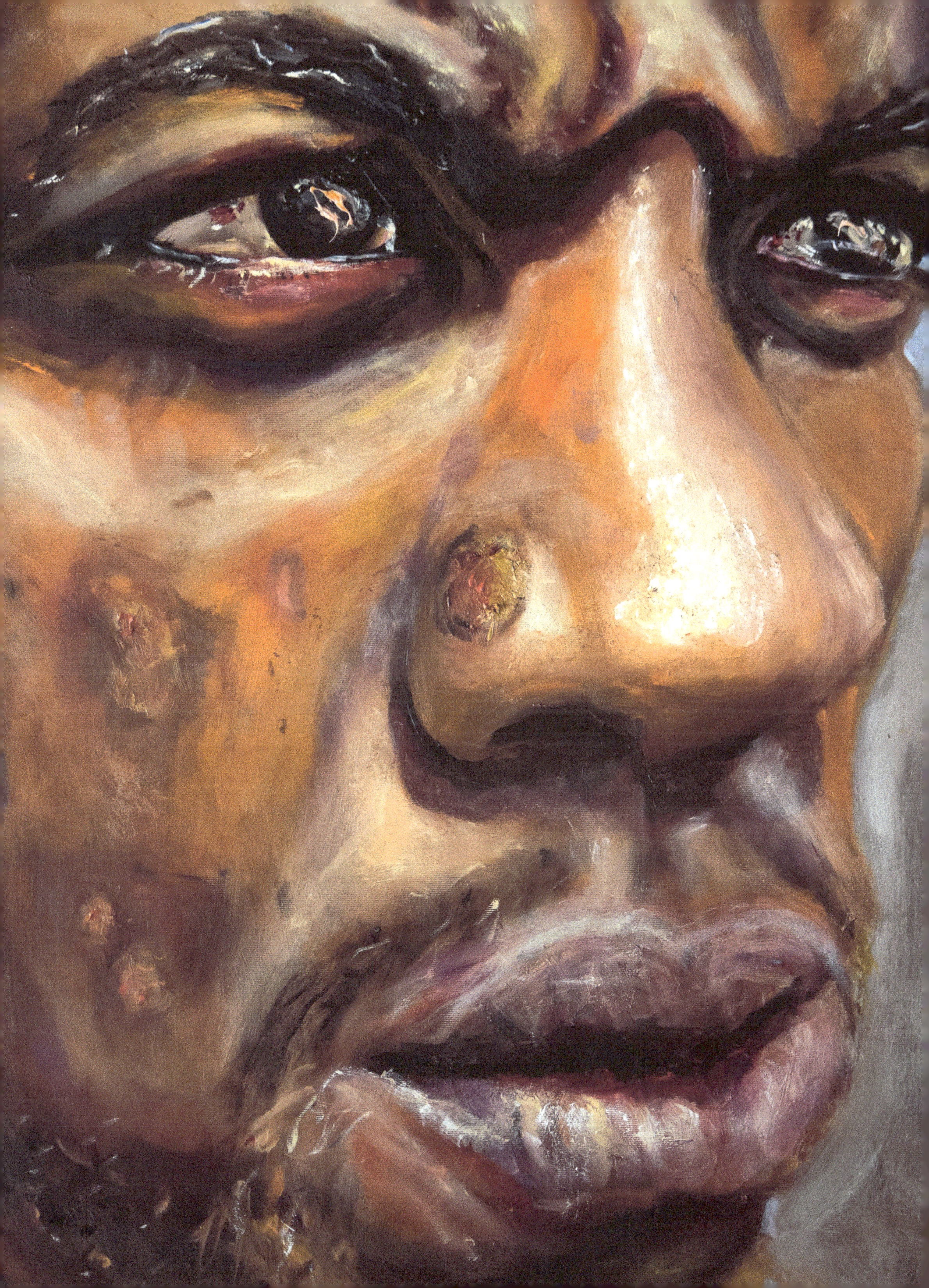

Crystal

When Crystal, 26, was 12 years old she told her father that her stepbrothers were raping her; he responded by kicking her out of their house. Her mother, who she describes as being "out to lunch," and "a prostitute, drunk and drug addict," did nothing.

On the streets with nowhere to go, Crystal was exploited by a pimp. He forced her, at gunpoint, to take drugs. She soon became addicted and for a period of time was also a prostitute.

Crystal has lived mostly on the streets for the past 14 years. At the time of this portrait she and her boyfriend Corey were expecting a baby. Crystal tried to access homeless services, such as going to the health clinic for pre-natal care and standing in line to collect her General Relief assistance, but said that "being homeless is tough – even finding a place to store my stuff when going to appointments is a struggle."

Social Services took the baby away after it was born, leaving Crystal "devastated." She finds it too painful to talk about. I've seen her many times since, still homeless on the beach.

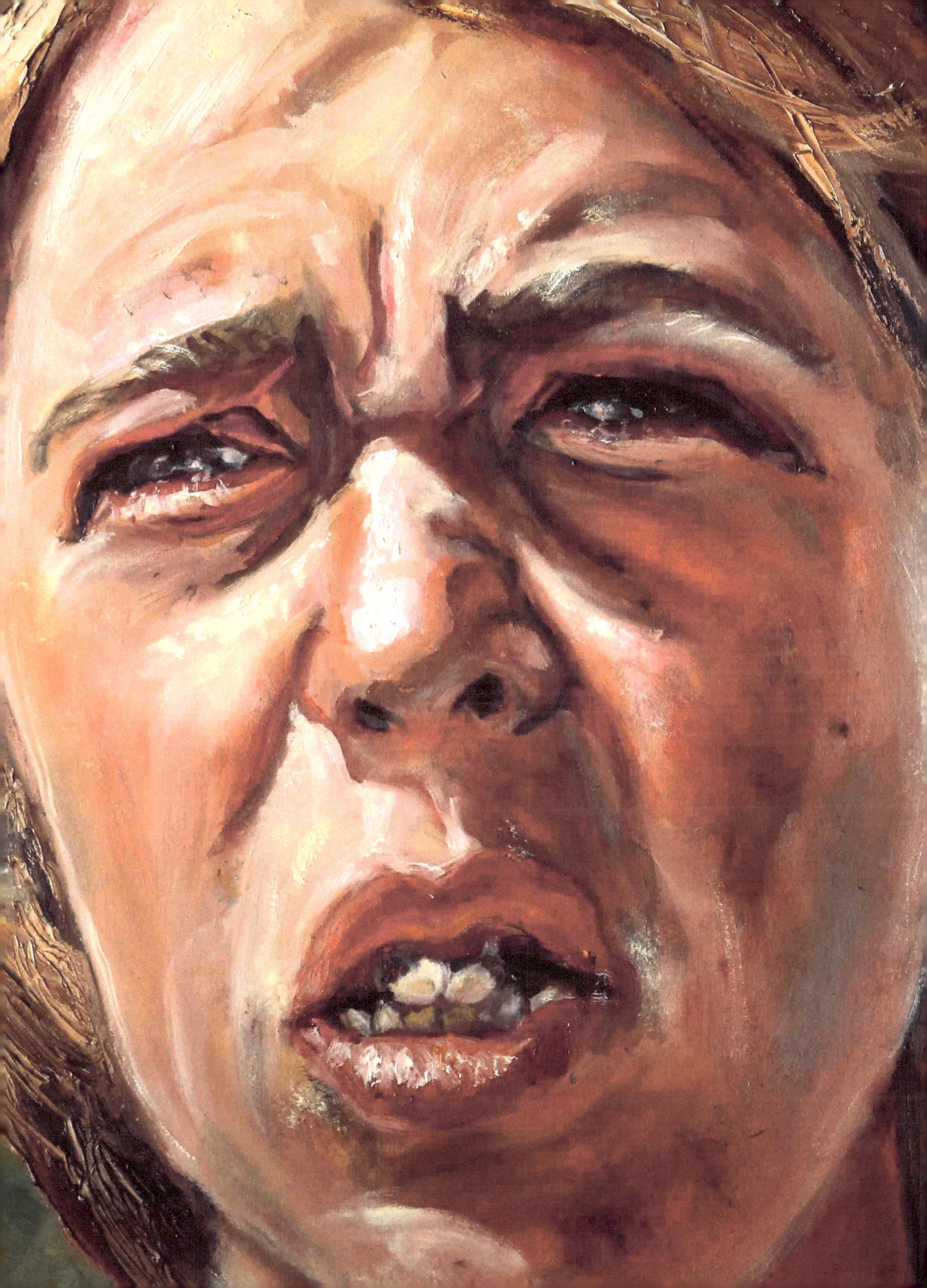

Ronald

Ronald, 65, was born in Alabama in an era where "KKK lynching of blacks was not uncommon." He recalls that it was "very scary to be black" at that time and "there was a lot of racism."

Ronald's parents taught him "right from wrong." Though they were very poor, they always made sure there was food on the table. But there was "violence in the family." Ronald did well in school, where he played many different sports and earned his GED. To help make ends meet, he worked as a dishwasher at age 15.

At the age of 19, Ronald joined the armed services and went to Vietnam. He "jumped out of planes into combat" and "watched people getting killed" all around him. He eventually went AWOL and was dishonorably discharged. When he came back from Vietnam it was very hard to get work.

Ronald has been homeless most of the time since then. He gets no veteran's benefits, though he does get Social Security assistance, given his age. Ronald cannot understand how this country can allow him and so many others to be homeless.

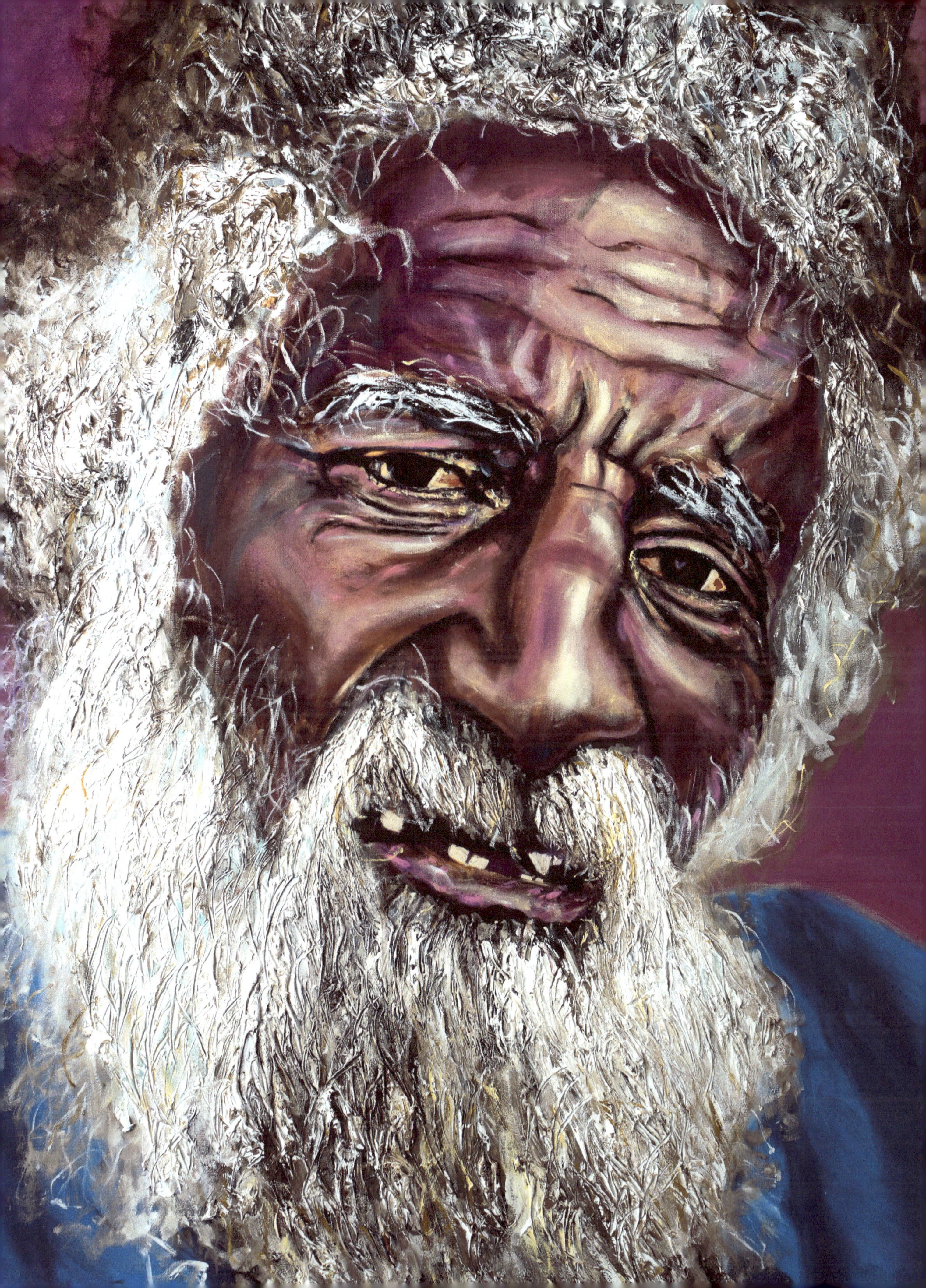

Wendy

Oil on Canvas
4' x 4'

Wendy, 46, is dying of stomach cancer. She cannot eat because she cannot keep anything down. And yet, she manages to look after and care for friends on Skid Row, many of whom call her "Mom."

Wendy's mother died when she was five years old, leaving her with an abusive father. When her grandmother died three years later her "life went to hell." Grandma was the only person who cared about her. At 14 the court emancipated Wendy from her father. There were no social services available to her so she dropped out of school and became a prostitute. She felt this was the only way to survive. She has had two abusive husbands, lost two children to a drunk driver, and has been on the streets, addicted to crack, for 20 years.

Wendy just wants to be happy, but that has eluded her: "God doesn't seem to want me to be happy. I'm still really a child, a child still wanting to learn to live and love."

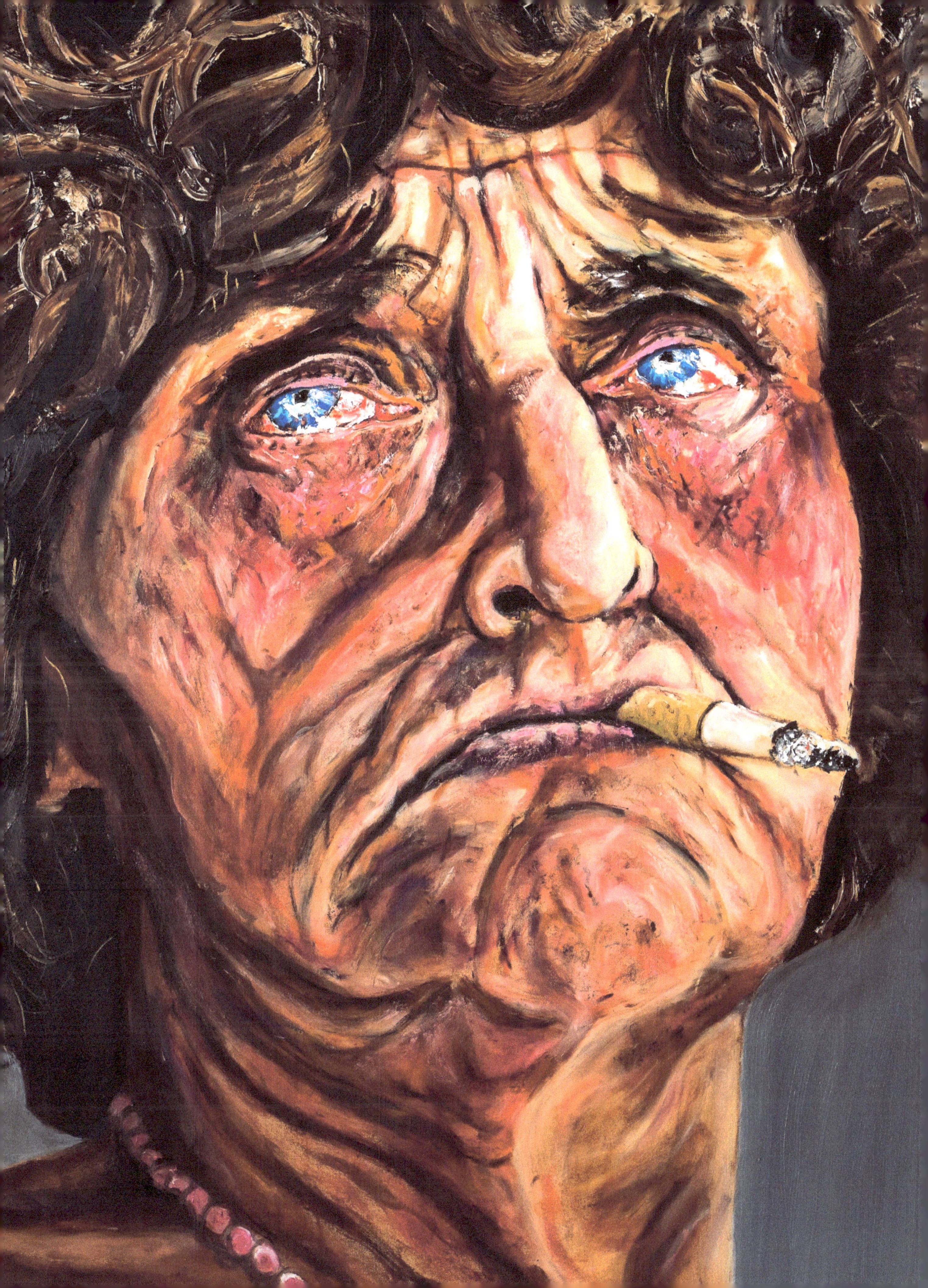

Jennifer

Born in Alabama, Jennifer, 43, started having seizures when she was three years old. This resulted in her missing so much school that by ninth grade she dropped out completely. It was not until ten years ago, at the age of 33, that Jennifer was properly diagnosed with diabetes. Once she got that under control, her seizures stopped.

Jennifer moved to Los Angeles as a young adult and worked as a college custodian and in the field of manufacturing and assembly. But in 2010, she became homeless when her long-term relationship ended and she had no money to support herself. Now Jennifer has "trouble with addictions" and is suffering from cancer. She needs surgery but has been told she is not strong enough to survive it at this time.

Jennifer wants to apply for benefits and get her "life in order," but cannot find the energy to move forward. Despite these hardships, she said of the portrait sitting: "Having someone listen to me and do a portrait was the best."

Two years after painting her portrait, I found Jennifer and gave her the print of her painting. I told her that her portrait was hanging in the office of Los Angeles Mayor Eric Garcetti. She responded, "I don't deserve it! I can't believe it! Thank you so much! Thank you, God, for sending someone who believes in us! I am going to send it to my father. Thank you from the bottom of my heart!" She then kept hugging me and cried deeply. It was like she was released from feeling like she was nothing.

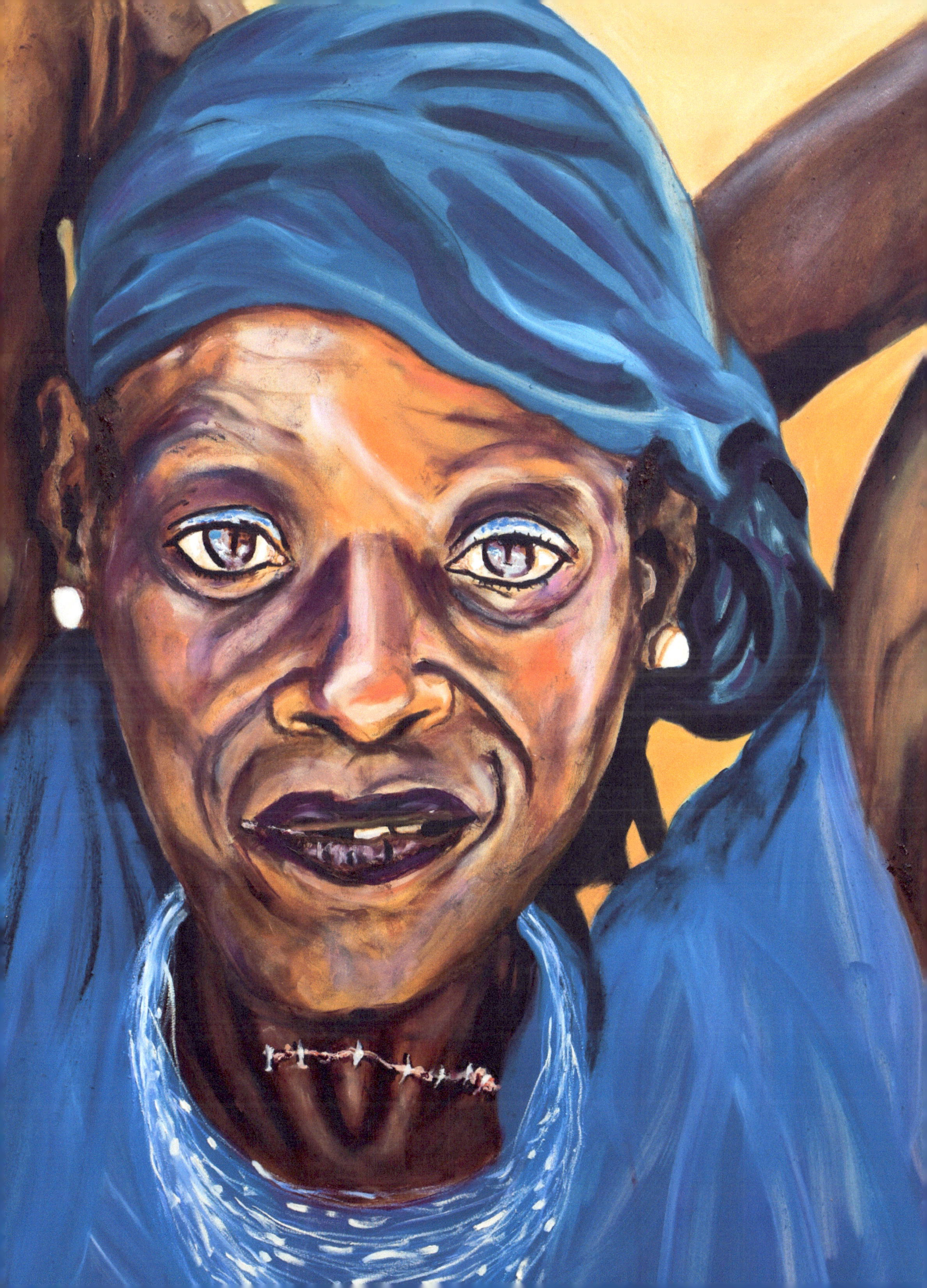

Mark

According to Mark, 54, his face shows us "the story of his life." The puss running out of Mark's eye made me feel nauseated.

Mark was born in South Dakota to a mother who was a go-go dancer, drug addict, alcoholic and prostitute. She raised four boys, with three different fathers. Mark never knew his father. Though life was chaotic, Mark deeply loved his mother.

Mark got his high school diploma and then went to trade school and became a mechanic. Hoping to make better money, he moved to Colorado Springs to work in the gold mines where he was a "powder monkey," delivering explosives. The smoke and blast fragments damaged his eyes and he has had difficulty finding work ever since. He is now blind, and his eyes are infected.

Mark took care of his mother for the many years she suffered from cancer. When she died in 1994, he lost everything and became homeless. Mark's ID was stolen, making it difficult for him to connect with governmental services. Over the years I continue to see Mark bereft on the beach.

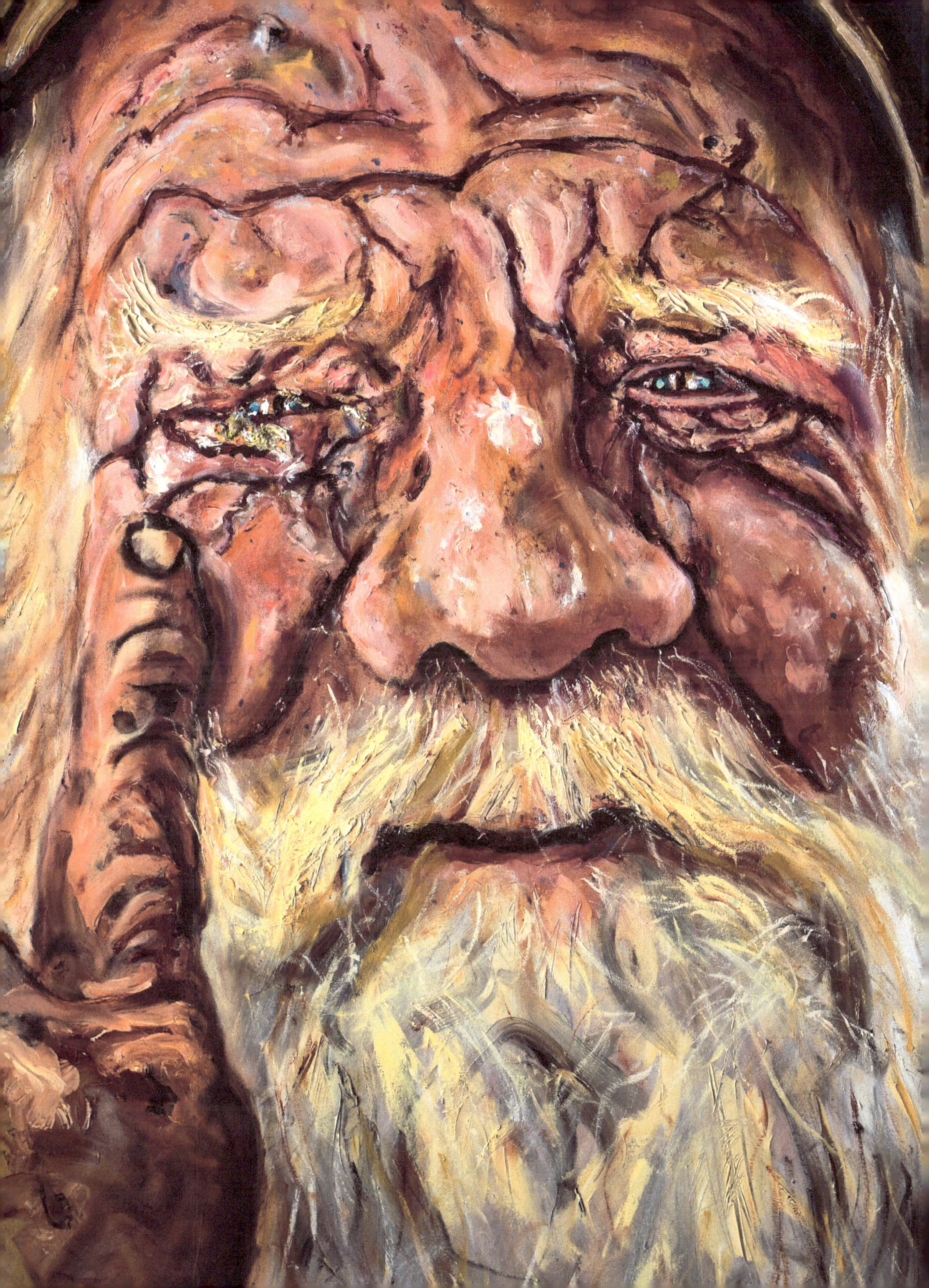

Pebbles

Pebbles, 27, wears her hair in a Mohawk and looks like a tough guy who could beat people up. She has a tattoo of an eagle on her chest and is a chain-smoker. But I soon got to know the sweet, intelligent person that she is.

Tears ran down her face as she talked about her mom, who was just 16 years old when Pebbles was born. Pebbles told me her mother took every drug in the book to abort her. Pebbles was actually born dead "for 15 minutes," so she has brain damage and a brain disease. Her brain is "currently eating away at itself" which causes her to behave like she's autistic. This could also be the reason she is severely dyslexic. Pebbles can't read a book but is very bright. Her memory is going and "Alzheimer's is probably going to kick in soon." Pebbles was institutionalized from the age of seven to nineteen, only allowed out one day per month. She has been in jail multiple times since then.

When Pebbles felt she could trust me, she told me her mother's boyfriends molested her from an early age. Her mother blames her for seducing these men. This is so painful for Pebbles because all she ever wanted was to be close to her mother.

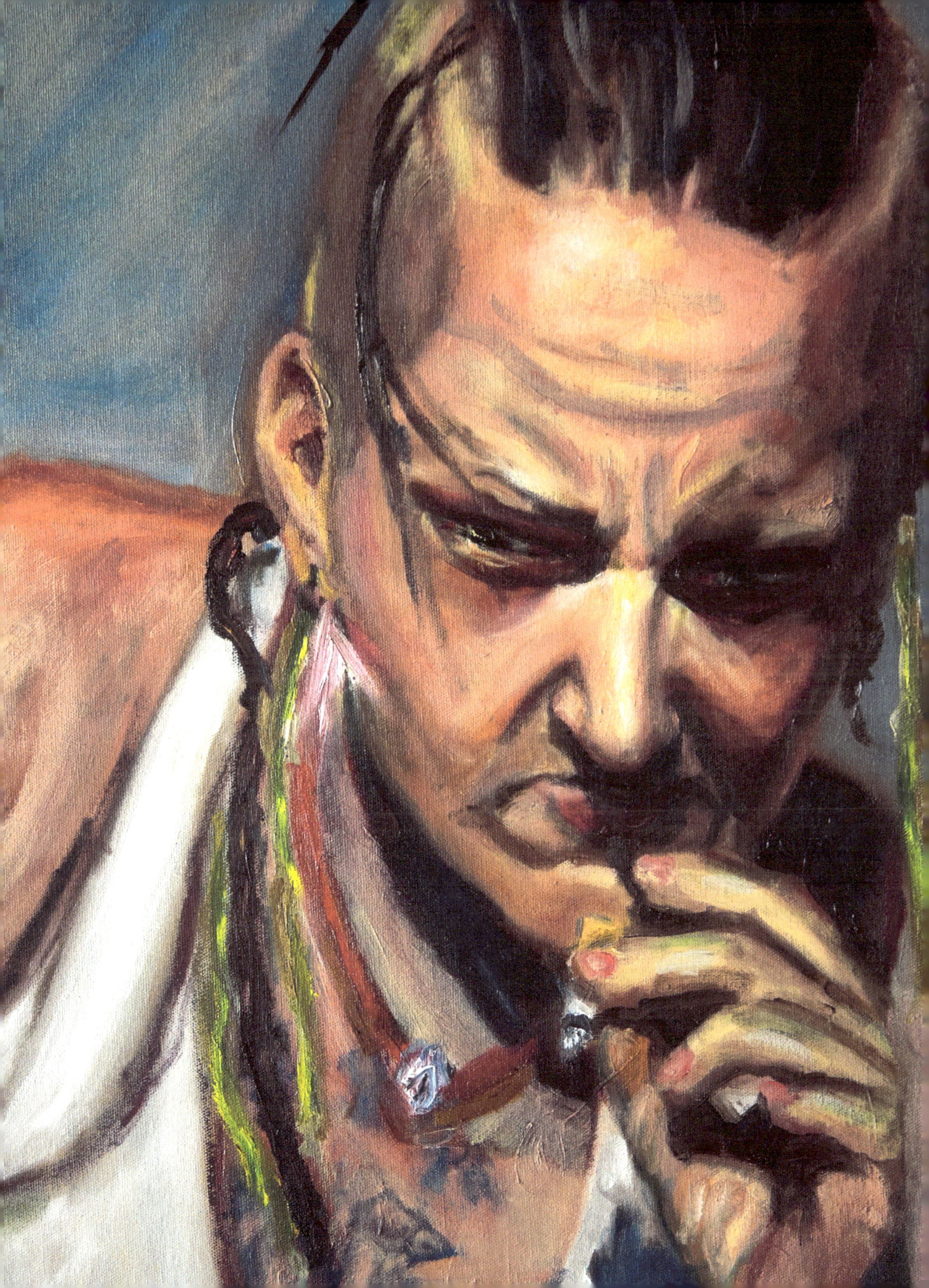

Dougie

Dougie, 50, spent most of his childhood being shuffled around the foster care system. When he was old enough, he decided to join the military. A veteran of the Gulf War, Dougie served as a Gunnery Sergeant in the Marines. His specialty was explosives.

One day during his tour in Kuwait, Dougie was sweeping for land mines. He stepped on one and in the explosion that followed he lost a leg. Since the time of Dougie's honorable discharge for his debilitating injury he has been "mostly homeless."

Dougie says that he has not been able to get any help from the VA because "there are just too many hoops to deal with." But even now, Dougie maintains that he would be willing to go back to war to protect this country, because he "believes in it." Dougie oversees and cares for a group of people living on the beach.

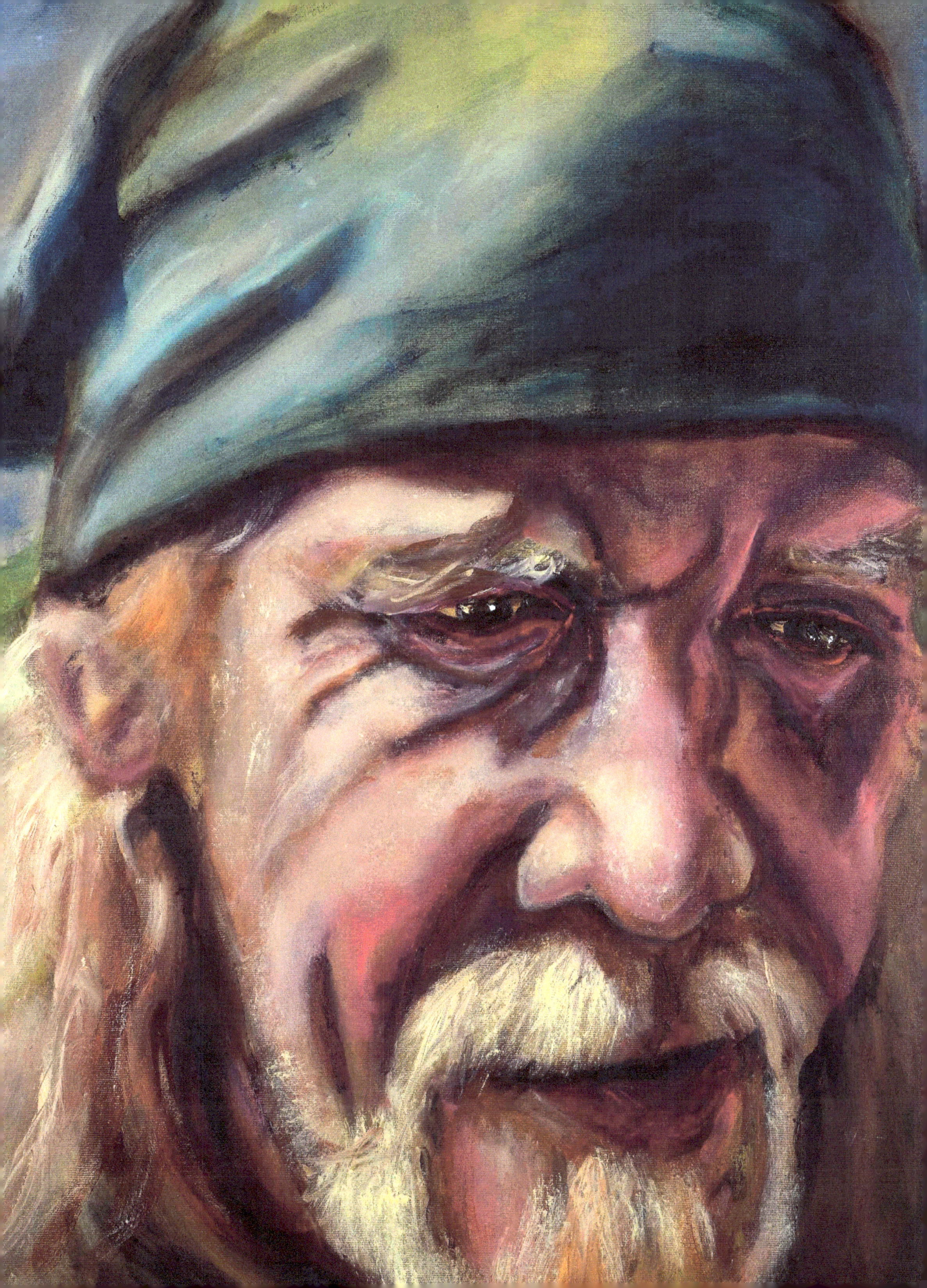

Black Crow

Oil on Canvas
3' x 3'

Black Crow, 49, is very proud of having been born on the reservation to parents who were Native American Dakota Sioux. Her father was a cross-country truck driver and her mother was an inspector of aircraft motors. But both parents were alcoholics and her father beat her mother.

When she was in seventh grade, Black Crow's parents divorced and everything in her life fell apart. She dropped out of school because "the chaos at home made it impossible to focus." That's when her sister gave her her first shot of heroin. Black Crow has been addicted ever since. When she was 16 years old, she became homeless.

Black Crow spends her days in a wheelchair on Skid Row. She cannot walk because she lost one leg to a bone infection and her knee replacement in the other leg is infected as a result of her drug use. She is on disability. Though registered as a Native American, she does not receive those benefits.

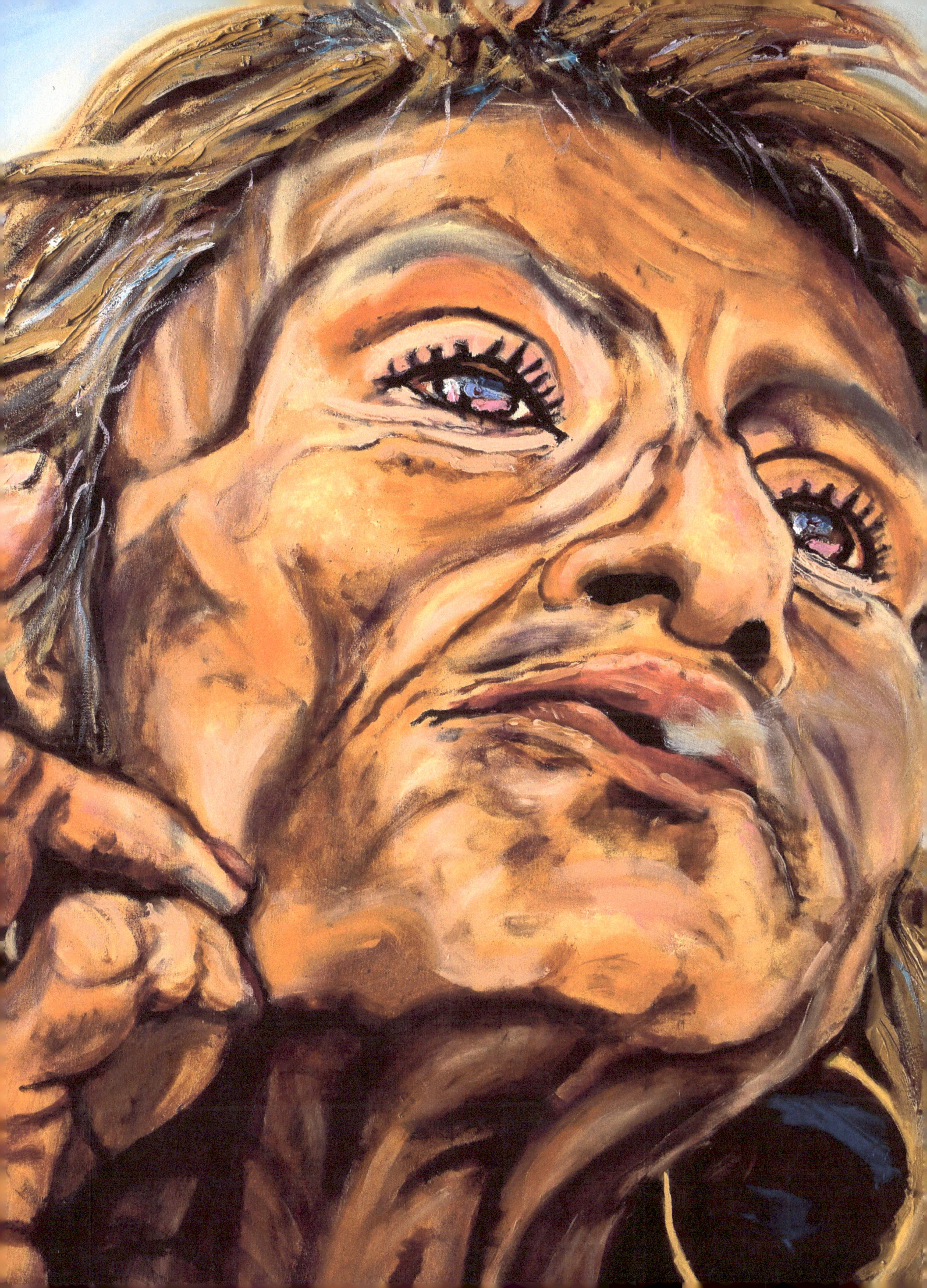

de La Barca

*Oil on Canvas
3' x 3'*

Born in El Salvador, de La Barca, 50, came to this country as a young man to escape the intense violence of civil war that surrounded him. He is a survivor of years of child abuse at home, wherein assaults with "belts, fire, wood, pots and pans" were common. He spent most of his youth fearing for his life.

Once in Los Angeles, de La Barca had good jobs and was "a workaholic." He was married for 15 years and had "many nice things." But one day, on his way to work at a paint company where he mixed and matched colors, he was hit by a car and broke his collarbone. He then learned that his wife was cheating on him. Between his heartbreak over the relationship and his inability to work due to his injury, de La Barca "deteriorated." He became an alcoholic and has been homeless on and off for many years.

De La Barca supports himself by selling the paintings he creates while living on the beach.

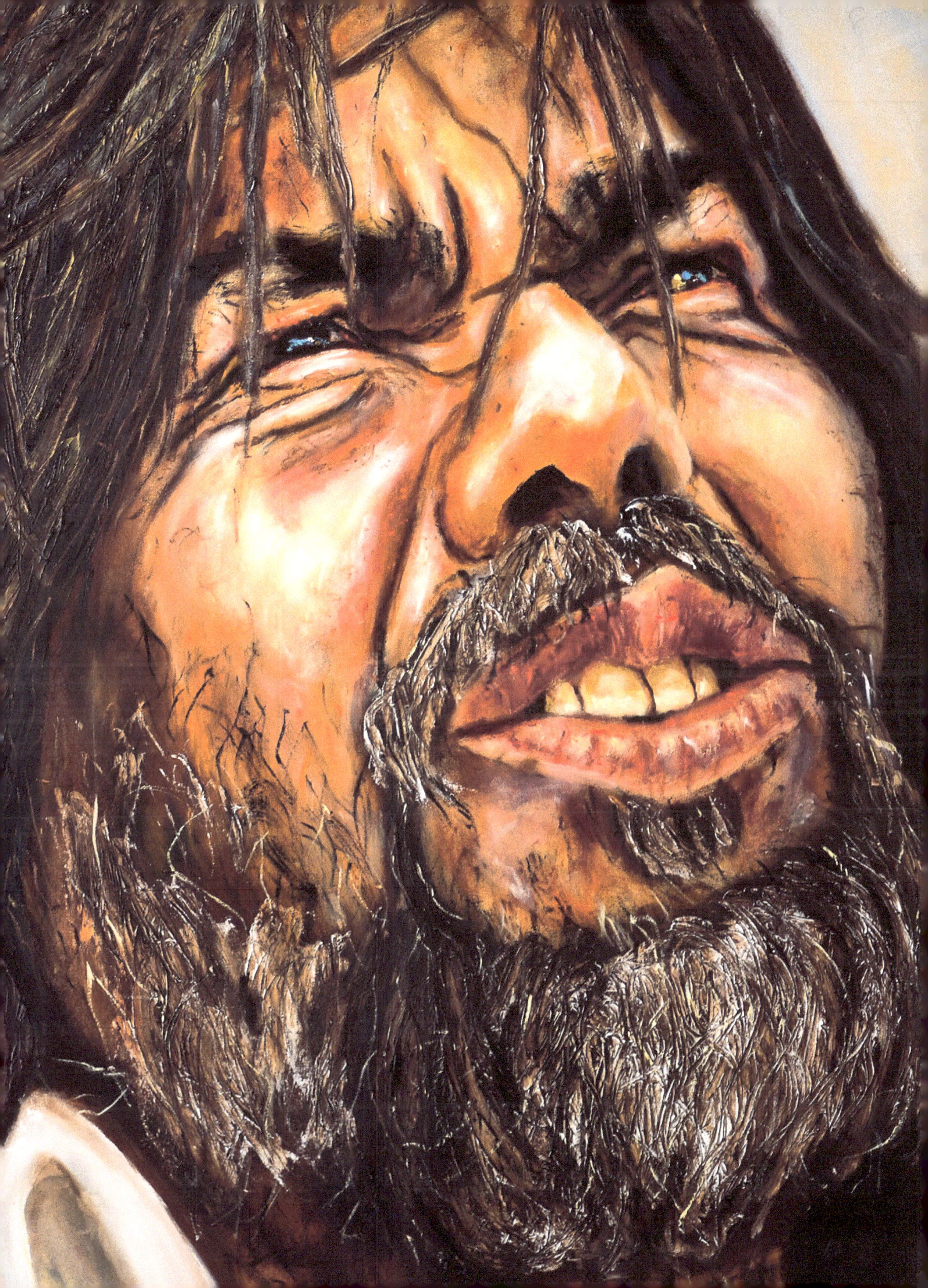

Annie

Oil on Canvas
18" x 24"

When I first saw Annie, 24, she was sitting with a German dictionary and books trying to teach herself how to read and speak German. Annie wants to be a children's book writer or a songwriter and wants to go to college and have a better life.

Annie has one of the worst reported histories of people experiencing homelessness I have interviewed. Annie was born to a mother who beat her, tortured her, and treated her like a slave. Annie showed me burns on her feet where her mother would put out cigarettes. Annie reports being raped repeatedly from the time she was eighteen months old. Once she was so bloodied by a babysitter that her mother had to rush her to the hospital. Annie "fell prey" to many people when unsupervised.

In her teens Annie was "dumped" by her mother at her father's house, but he kicked Annie out onto the streets. At age 17 she was raped and had a baby. This baby is the most important thing in Annie's life. But she has not been able to gain custody of the child.

Annie says she continues to be raped while living on the beach. She feels claustrophobic, mistrustful of all people, fearful of love and convinced that people will hurt her because almost everyone has. She has to drug herself to sleep.

Annie recently had a new baby which was taken away by social services, and it broke Annie's heart once again. Over the years I continue to see her living on the beach.

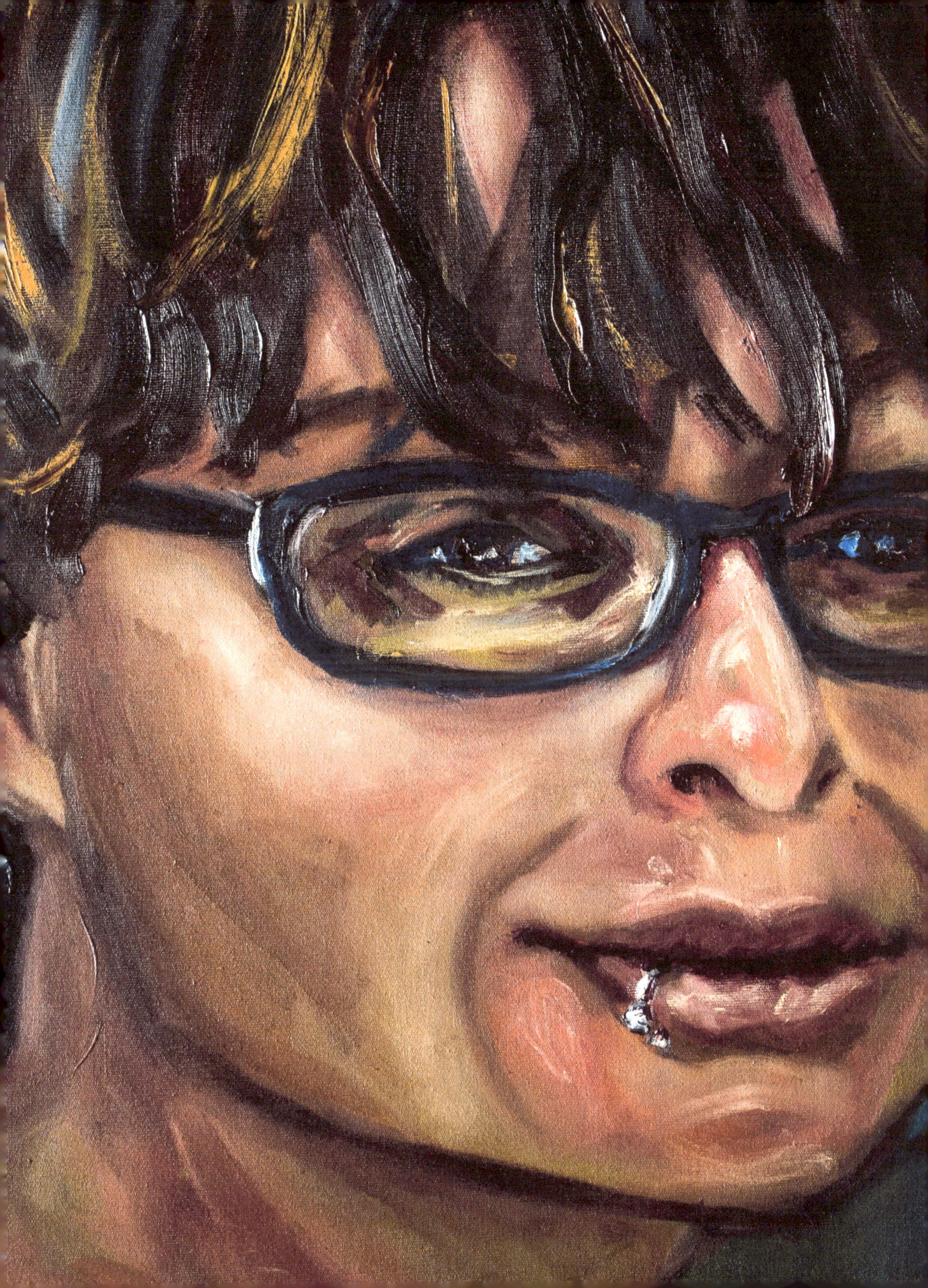

Coco

Coco, 32, a stunningly good-looking redhead, is transgender. Born a male, she is taking hormone shots and other measures to fully become a woman. She says she has always felt like "a woman trapped in a man's body."

Coco was born to "a rich divorce attorney mother and an ex-gang banger father" who was many years sober. Coco excelled in school, was wildly popular, and played football as a halfback and defensive-end at a prestigious high school. She had "a very spoiled and protected childhood with all the advantages money could buy." She recalls being the only black person in many social situations.

Though never attracted to women, Coco dated extensively. She tried desperately to hide who she really was and to pass as a heterosexual male. While her mother is now supportive financially, Coco feels the only place in the world where she is fully accepted and can be her true self is on Skid Row: "I've been fighting my whole life to get respect from people and society." Coco is often called a "crazy bitch" and has been physically attacked many times because of how she's trying to live her life.

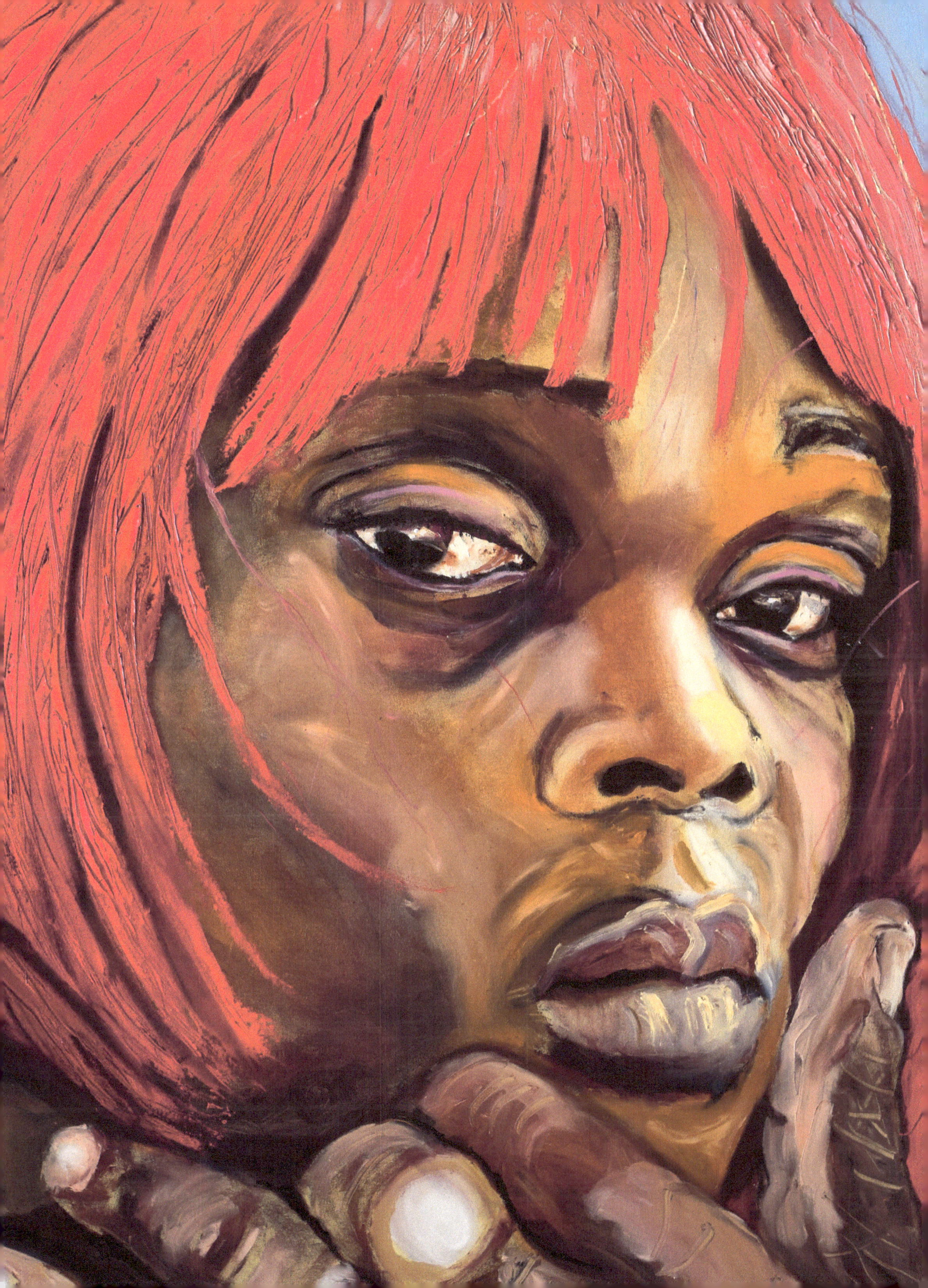

Father/Daughter

The subjects of this portrait must remain anonymous. They are among the many families with children of all ages living on the beach and on the streets who feel they need to be invisible. If the authorities know they are homeless, they will try to take the children away and place them in foster care or wherever they deem to be better living conditions. According to this father, that only breeds fear and distrust, discouraging him and others from seeking services.

Many of these families try to keep their children in school, but this is not always possible given the harsh realities of their existence.

In this situation the father eventually gave the baby to the mother's parents to raise. He is still trying to find a way to earn enough money to get his daughter back. I hired him to help me with this project so he could make a few extra dollars.

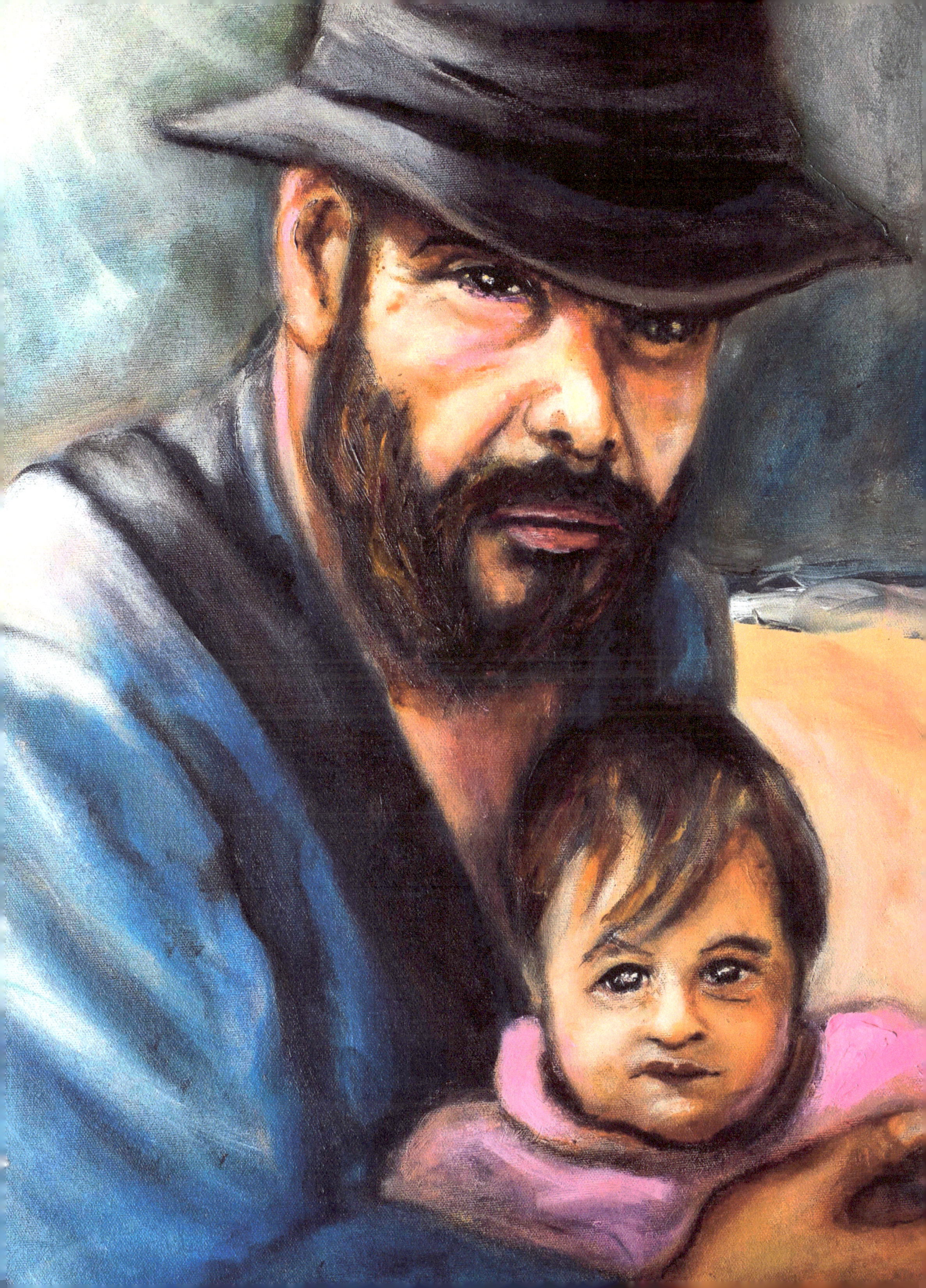

Raleigh

Each time I saw Raleigh on the beach as I was painting others, we would chat a bit and then he would ask if I would paint him next; each time I told him that I had put him on the list. Though only in his 60s, Raleigh looked to be in his 70s. He was always sitting very still, and wore a ski cap no matter how hot the weather. I soon learned that he had a terrible case of asthma and that whenever he tried to breathe it was "a real life-and-death struggle."

Raleigh was born in Tennessee and raised in Texas, the product of a one-night stand. He lived with his mother, who he described as "all right." He wanted to grow up to be a cowboy but instead he worked on shrimp boats, in construction, cutting lawns, doing carpentry and loading trucks. He says he liked the period of his life when he was a singer in a heavy metal band.

Raleigh did not reveal much about what led to his homelessness. He told me he gets in angry moods and tends to get into fights; sometimes in these fights he has been seriously injured. Once he was hit in the head and his skull was crushed - I wondered if this was why he always wore his cap. To me he seemed to show symptoms of brain damage.

When our portrait session was completed, Raleigh thanked me and said the painting experience made him "feel like Jesus Christ for a day."

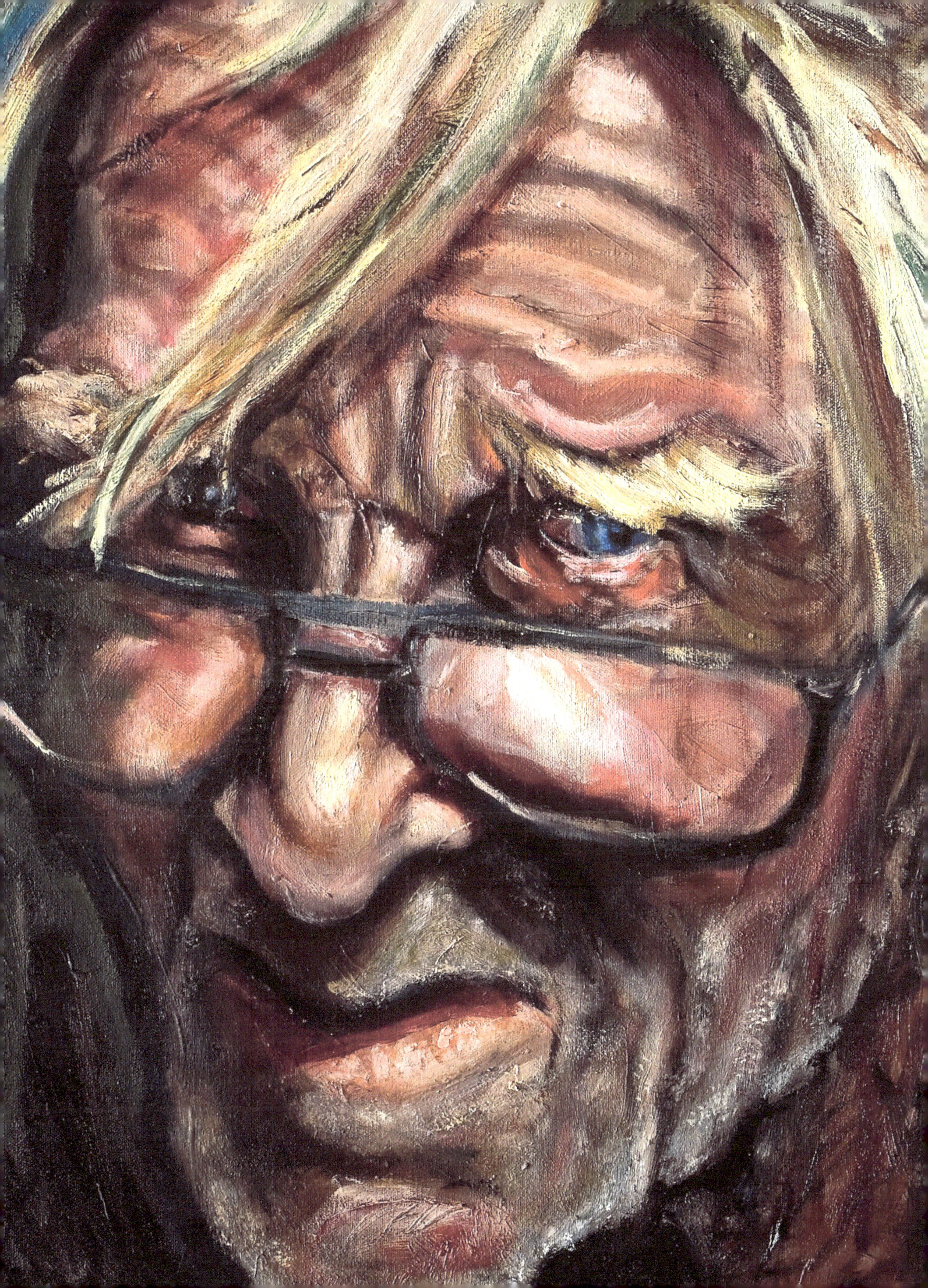

Andrew

Raised in Dallas by a single mother, Andrew, 65, was one of 10 children. He reveals little about his childhood except to say that it, like most of his life, was "filled with violence." Andrew's mother was a nurse and a housekeeper. She was also an artist and she taught Andrew to draw.

Andrew dropped out of school when he was in seventh grade because he had trouble learning to read and was told he was "retarded," but he continued to draw. Through the years he has sold paintings and has had solo exhibitions in galleries.

Andrew seems haunted by a tragedy that occurred when he was eight years old. One day he and his friends were playing and they ran across the street to hide in some bushes. Unbeknownst to them, a little three-year-old girl from the neighborhood was following close behind. As she chased after them, a car struck and killed her. Andrew continues to relive this horror and remains plagued by guilt 57 years later.

Andrew has been on the streets on and off for the last 40 years. His leg "gave out" eight years ago and he has been in a wheelchair ever since.

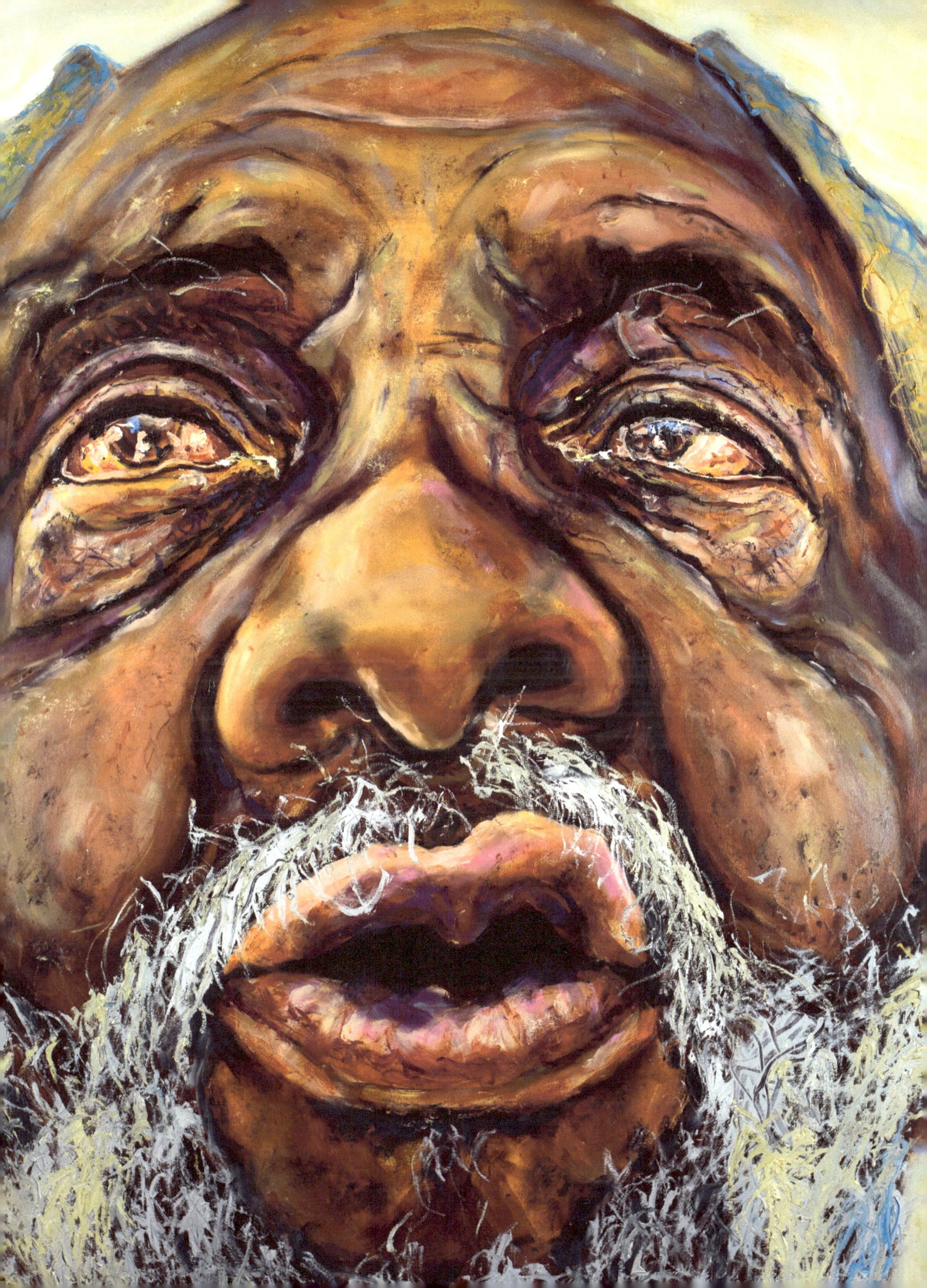

Latosha

Oil on Canvas
3' x 3'

Latosha, 29, got out of prison two years ago, where she had been serving five years for brutally stabbing her abusive girlfriend. The attack was so violent that her girlfriend was on life support for several months before recovering.

Though Latosha initially painted her childhood as being "very nice," when I told her that people who do violent things to others usually have had some terrible past experiences, she admitted to being attacked with a knife when she was young in much the same way she attacked her girlfriend. She then went on to say that her father was "absent" and her mother was an alcoholic. She summed her life up: Simply: "Lots of bad things happened."

Latosha has an associate's certificate in child development and has been employed in the child care field. She has also worked in customer service at Jamba Juice. She receives no governmental support or governmental services. She now survives only "by the blessings of other people" who give her handouts. I continue to see her on the streets of Skid Row.

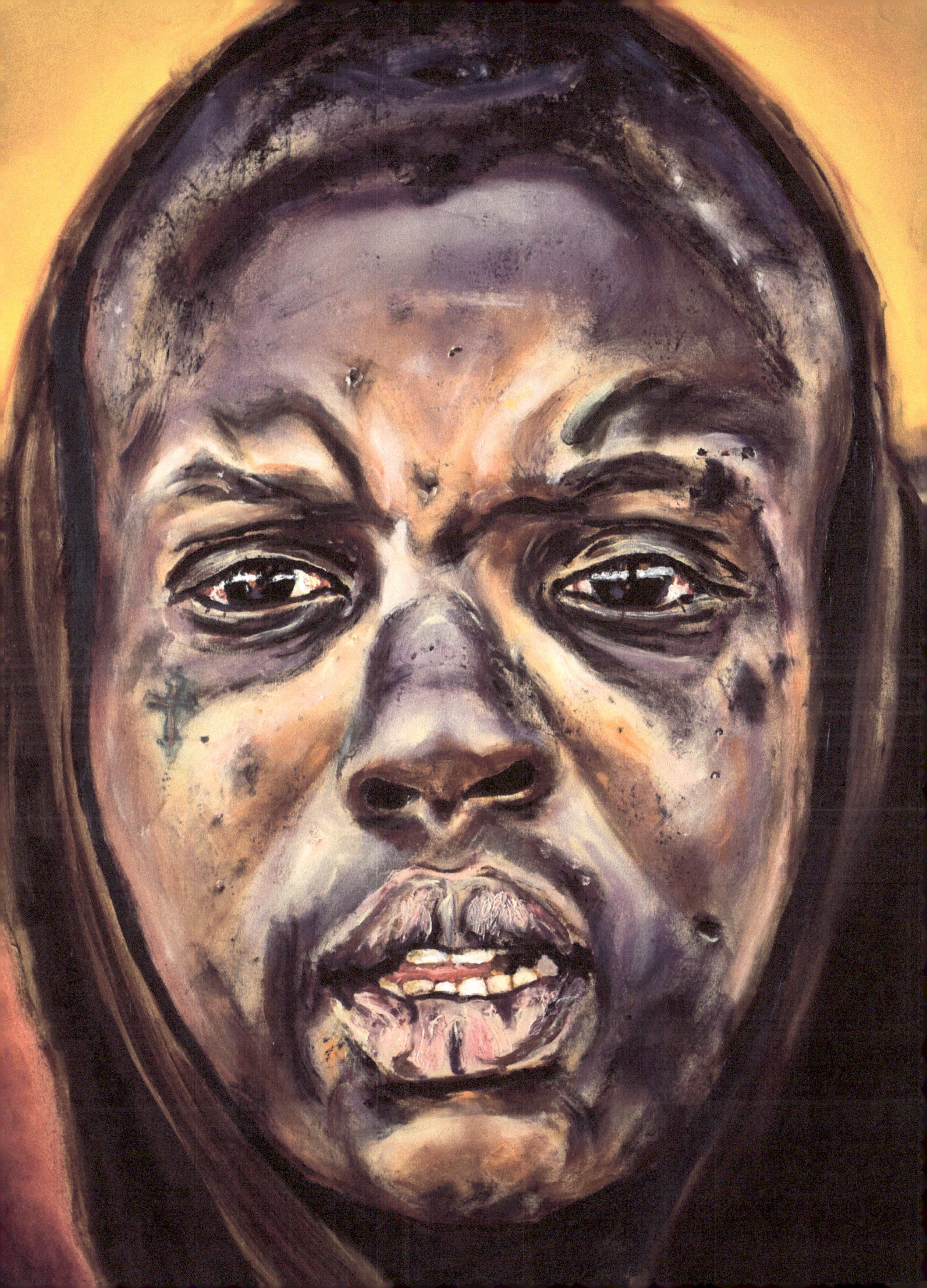

Shadow

Oil on Canvas
3' x 3'

Small, fast-talking and very smart, Shadow, 53, looks like a weathered leprechaun. He describes himself as an only child who was "pampered" by his parents. When speaking of his father, a guitar player, he cries. Shadow also played guitar, writing most of the songs for his band Fahrenheit, which he describes as "moderately successful." He wrote and played songs with Alice Cooper as well. Shadow then "went corporate," and became "very successful."

Things were good for a time, but then he "met [his] Waterloo." He lost most of his assets to his wife in their divorce and made some "bad business decisions." Then his biggest client's check bounced and Shadow lost everything. That was 15 years ago. He has been homeless ever since. He would like to get back on his feet but says it is hard. He earns some money making panhandling signs and selling them to tourists.

Shadow describes being homeless as the worst thing that ever happened in his life – he has been assaulted and spit on and feels like he's looked at "like a piece of trash."

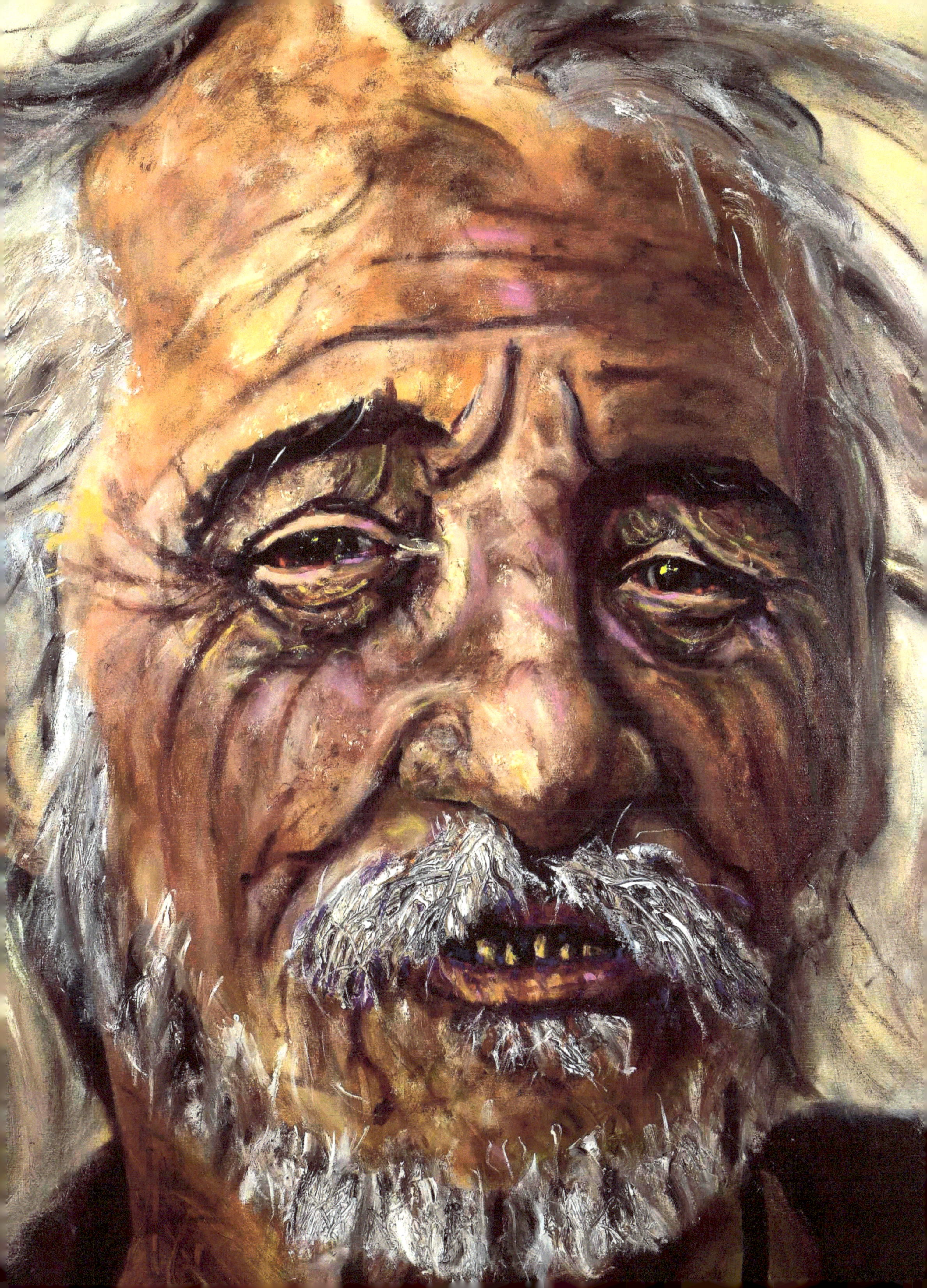

Black

Oil on Canvas
18" x 24"

Black, 20s, is a charming, shy guy with a big smile. He could not remember much about his early life but did tell me he grew up in Pomona in the foster care system, which he entered at age three. He didn't know his parents at all but he believes his father was 19 and his mother 15 when they had him. Black lived with three different foster families, which he said was rough, but he considers his last foster family his "real" family.

Black was incarcerated for two years for selling drugs. Prison was difficult but he told me it was a good experience because it made him grow: he "learned how to stay alive and not be reckless, to slow down and take one step at a time." Black sells jewelry on the beach for some income and usually sleeps there when he cannot crash on someone's couch.

As a result of our talks about his childhood, Black became interested in finding out more about his parents. He took the money I gave him for painting his portrait to buy a copy of his birth certificate. I saw Black on the beach for years.

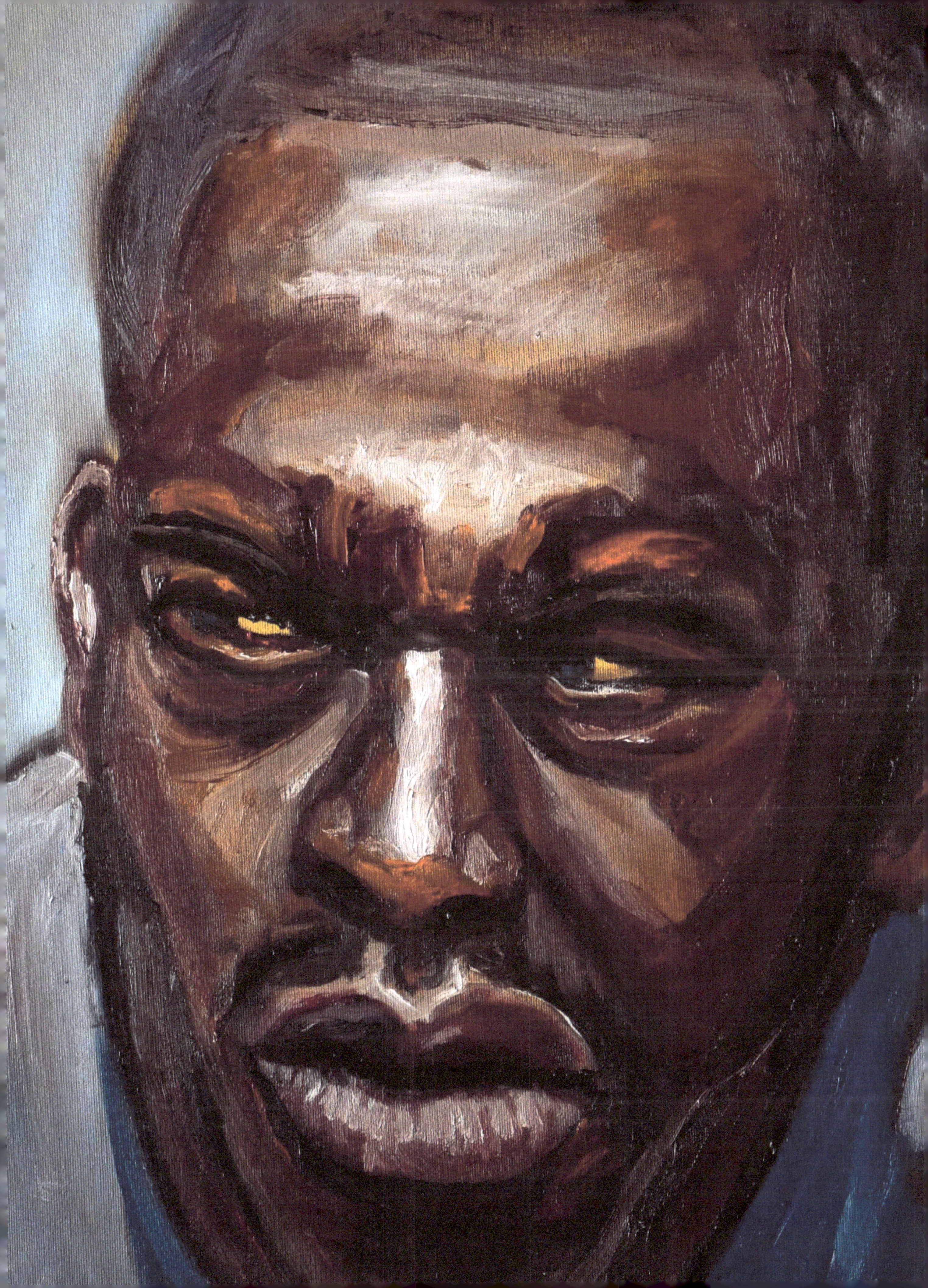

Christine

Christine, 32, insisted that we buy makeup before agreeing to sit for her portrait – perhaps to cover up scars on her forehead that were the result of one of her many abusive relationships. Together we walked half a mile while she pushed her cart to the store and then it took her 45 minutes to apply the makeup. By the time she was ready she had begun to shake - she needed a heroin fix.

Born in California, Christine was "picked on" in school but managed to graduate with a high school degree. She was a salesperson at Target, a waitress, bartender, a secretary, and now, a prostitute. She describes her mother as "evil," believing she tried to kill Christine because Christine was to inherit her grandfather's "money and beautiful house." Her mother also encouraged Christine's father to beat her frequently and fiercely. Of the abuse she has suffered over the years she says, "It's almost okay because that's all I've ever known."

Christine became homeless two years ago when she got "kicked out" of her house after her uncle, who was in prison for molesting children, was released. Christine survives on General Relief and food stamps.

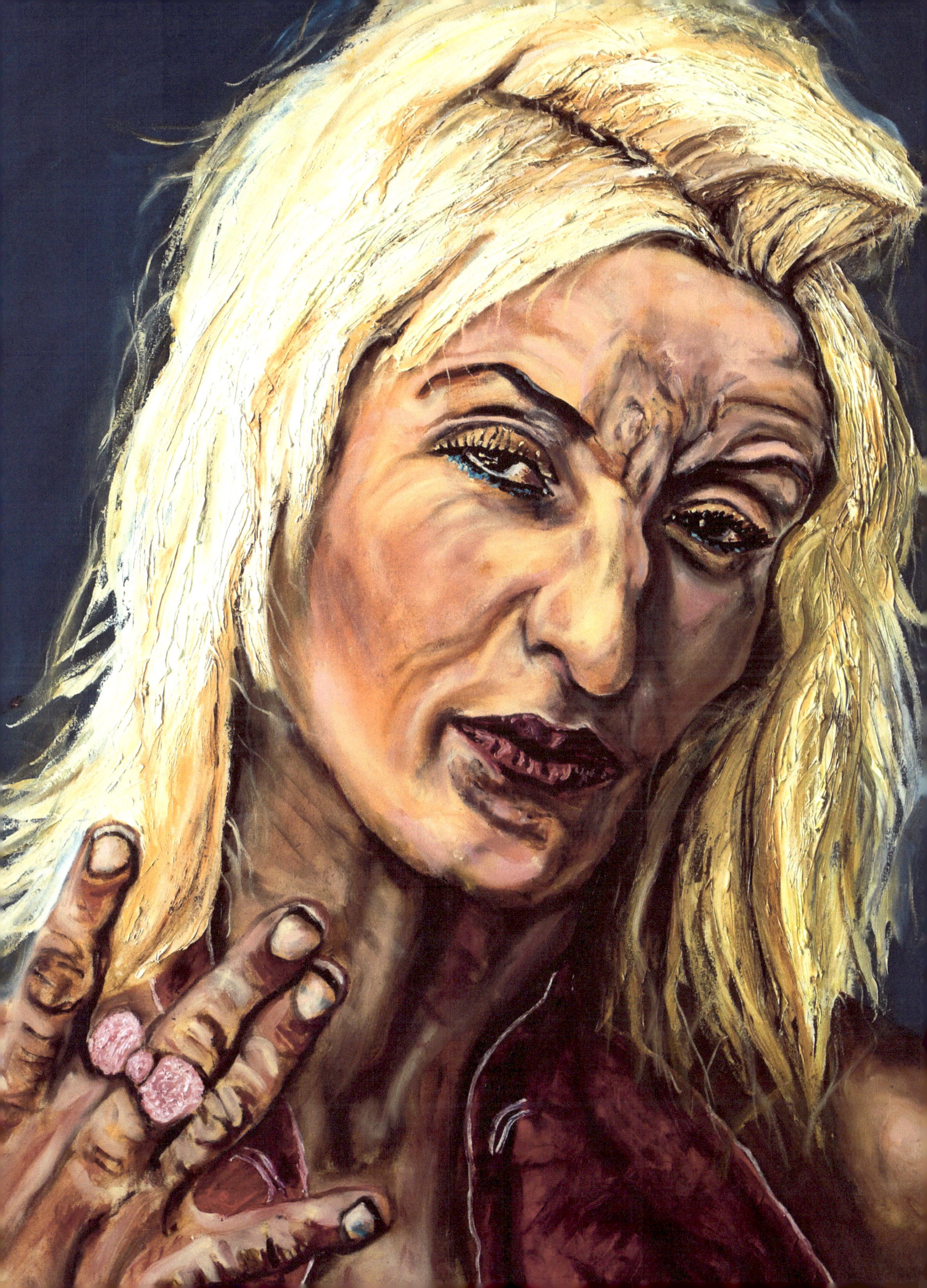

Doc

Sometimes when I was upset I would sit and talk with Doc. Doc, 50s, is an "urban camper" on the boardwalk. He likes the term urban camper because he thinks it's a sophisticated term for what he is doing. Doc is Cherokee and Blackfoot Indian, with a bit of Irish. He struck me as a very solid, intelligent, calm and personable guy.

Doc has two PhDs, one in nursing and one in psychology. He was a physician's assistant on death row in a southern border state. One of his jobs was to strap the person being electrocuted into the chair and ensure that he had died. After doing this for years Doc says he just couldn't do it anymore.

Doc sees Venice Beach as an antidote to death row. He told me he raised his children, paid his bills, bought a home and then gave his kids the house. Since the age of five, when he first saw the beach in Los Angeles, Doc has wanted to retire here. He has made friends with the police on the beach and feels they look out for him. Doc goes to church each Sunday and calls his daughter once a week.

Postscript: Four years after I painted his portrait, Doc died on the beach. His death rocked me. I spoke about him at a church service for him and others who recently died on the streets. His portrait and this bio were on display at the service.

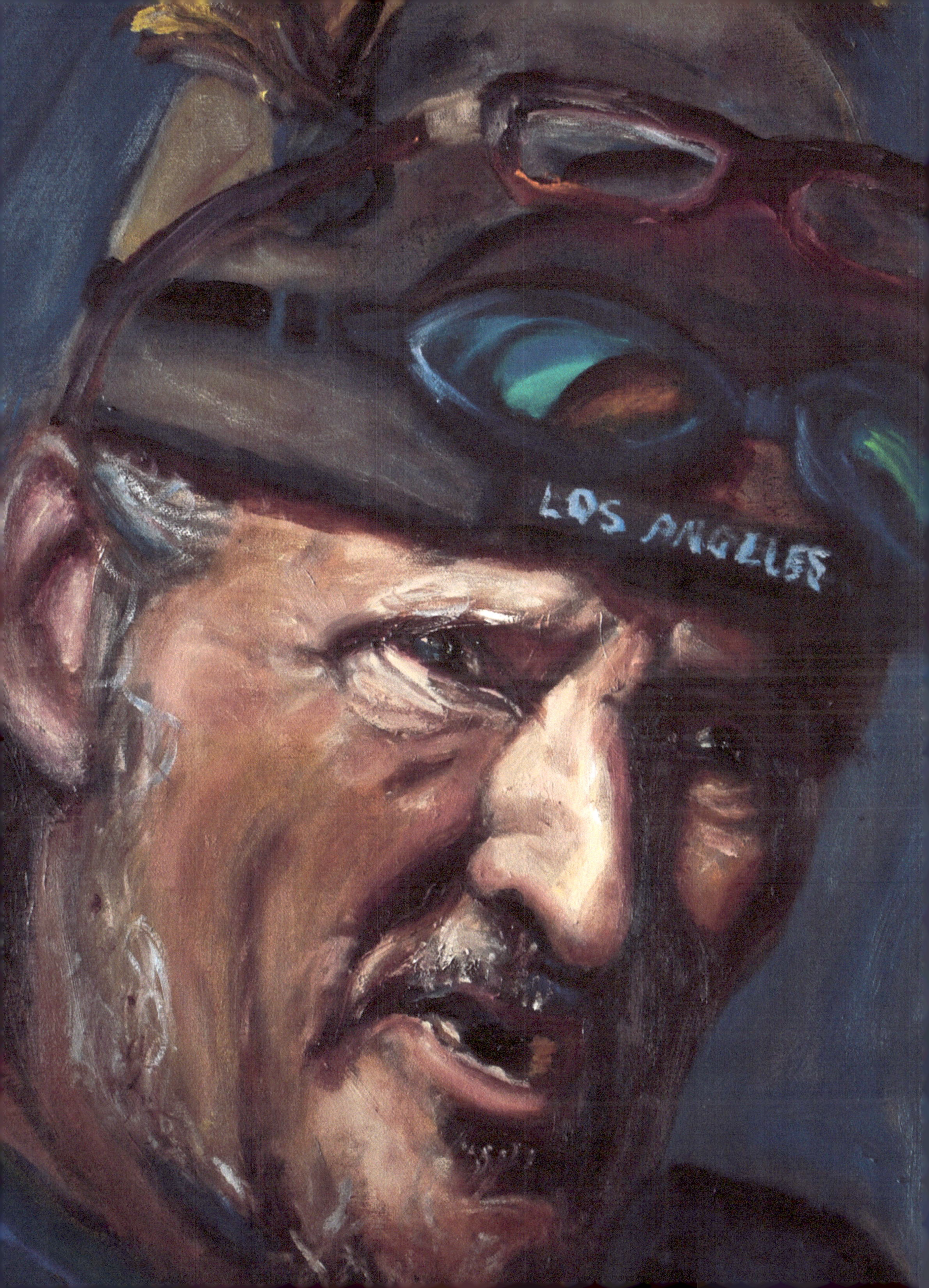
LOS ANGLES

Henry

Born to a heroin-addicted mother who left him at the hospital, and a father he never knew, Henry, 40, spent the first five years of his life in foster care. Then he was adopted by a family where he finally felt loved. The adoptive family was financially stable and successful until his adoptive father lost his job and "things fell apart."

Henry received a Master's in Public Administration from USC and was a city administrator overseeing major projects for years. But he had a secret. At 15, Henry hurt his back and was given narcotics and unlimited prescriptions for pain. He became addicted, and slowly transitioned to cheaper and more available street drugs. For a long time, Henry was able to keep his addiction from disabling him completely. But it slowly spiraled out of control. Eventually he realized it was interfering with his job, so he quit while still in good standing.

Henry met his wife of five years, Gen (next page), while in rehab. They have a daughter who now stays with Henry's adoptive father. Henry and his wife live on the streets and continue to be addicted to heroin. Both hope to kick the habit, get jobs and get their daughter back.

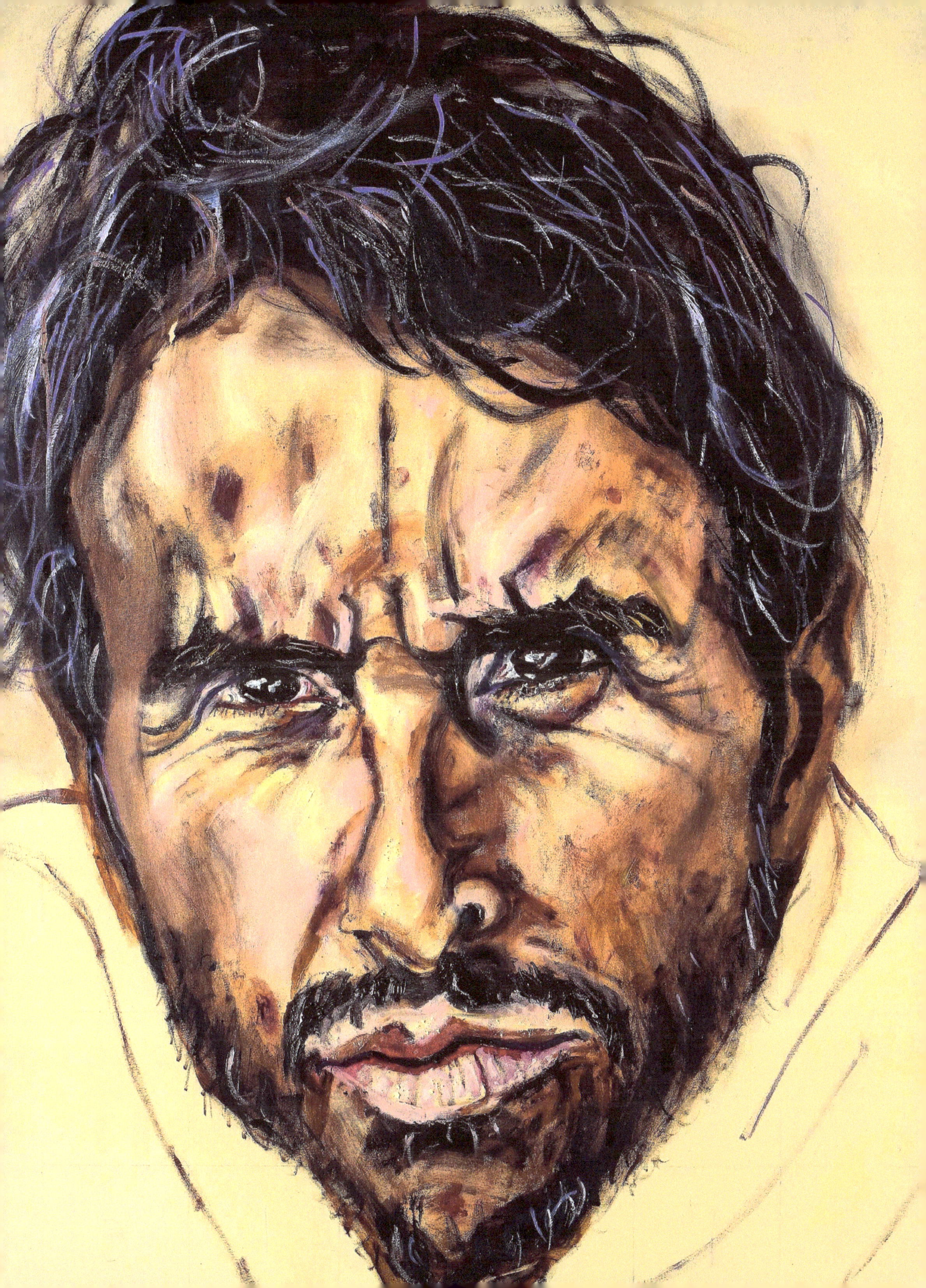

Gen

*Oil on Canvas
3' x 3'*

Gen, 34, lived an upper-middle-class life in Los Angeles – and she comes across that way. Her father was an extremely successful artist, but also an alcoholic who physically and emotionally abused her. Her mother was "mean" and "in denial" about her husband's behavior. Gen did well in school and enjoyed it. She has had some college, but never graduated.

Gen has been addicted to heroin for the last eight years. She's been in and out of rehab, but so far "it hasn't worked." She met her current husband, Henry, with whom she lives on Skid Row, in rehab. Though they tried to live with her family, the violence and abuse there led them back to the streets where "it's safer." They have been homeless for several months now and Gen receives General Relief and Medi-Cal.

Gen has a daughter with Henry (previous page), but she was taken away from them and is now being raised by Henry's adoptive father. She hopes to get her back one day and have a home. But Gen knows that she and her husband must first get jobs to do that.

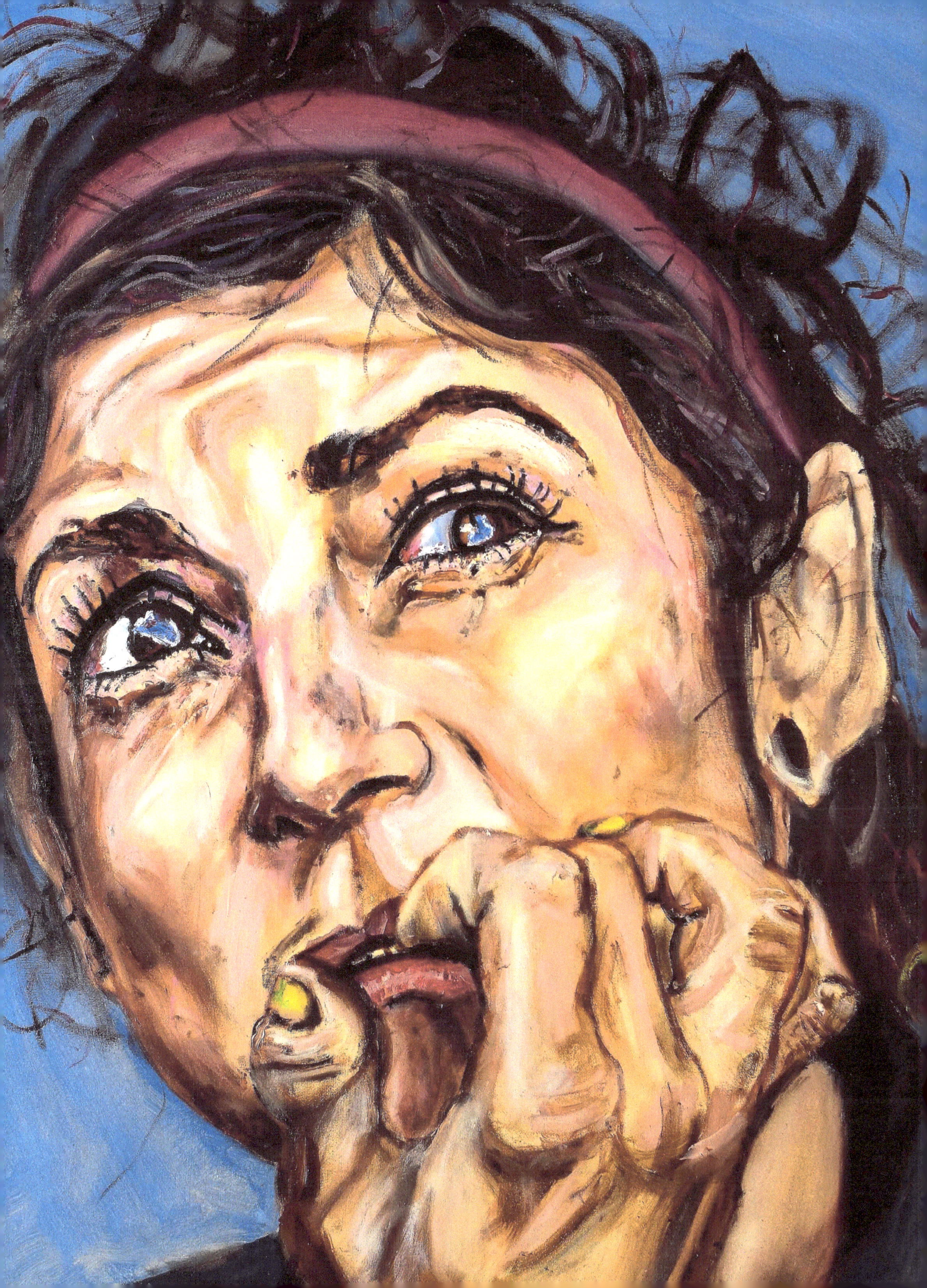

James

James, 59, was born in Louisiana, in a part of town where "poverty and violence were the norm." His father was an alcoholic who suffered from PTSD as a result of his service in WWII.

James was not a very good student and never graduated from high school. He struggled to find jobs. When nothing was available, he supported himself mostly through crime. He has spent years in and out of jail for burglary.

Due to a medical error during a hospital visit, James lost his leg. He has now lost hope and no longer has any goals. In many respects he seems to be just waiting to die.

James supports himself by "hustling" – these days that is mostly by selling Viagra. For any medical issues he calls 911. James is sad that his disability keeps him from being physically active, since that is what gave him the most joy in life.

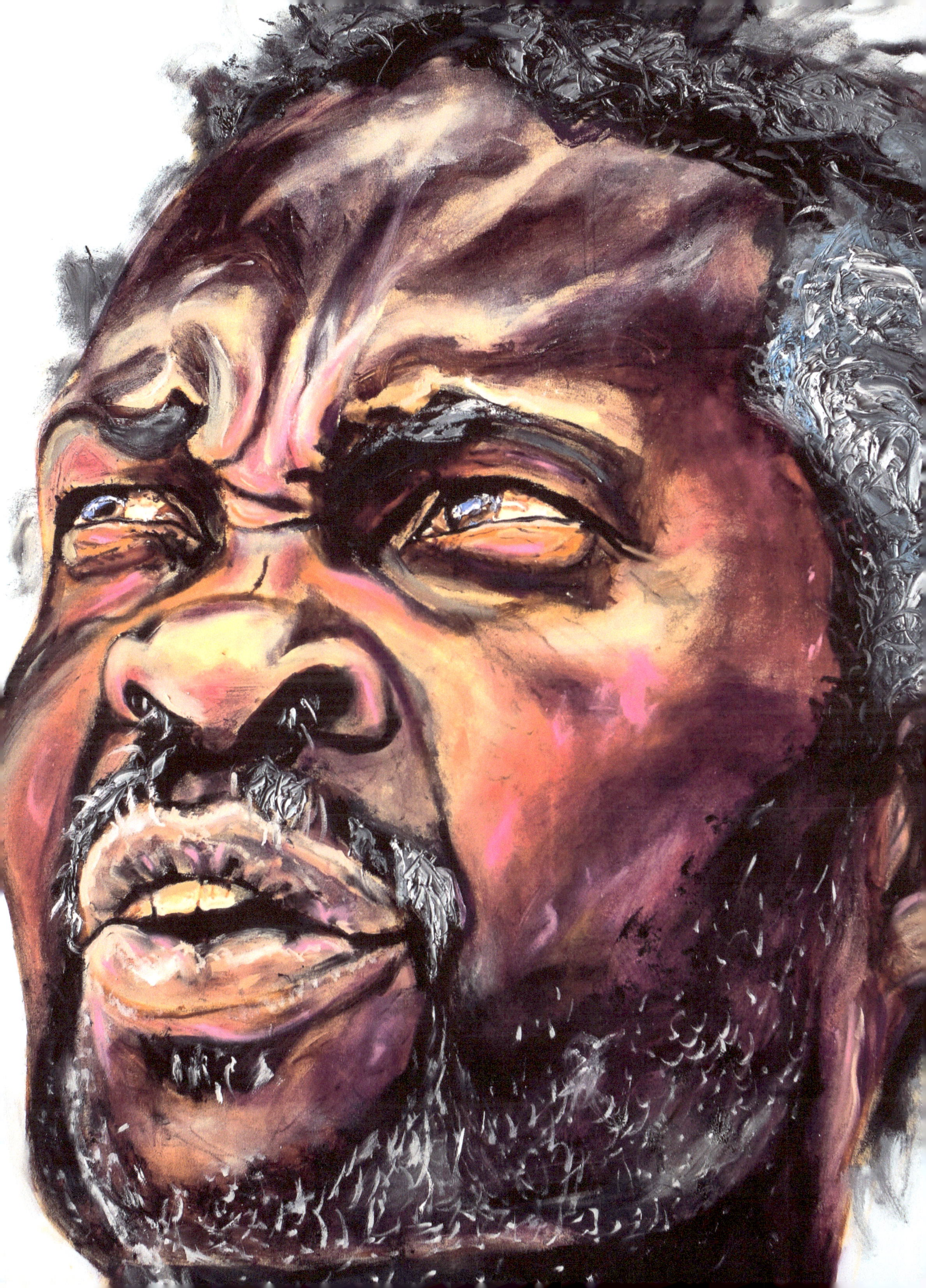

Flo

When Flo, 58, was 22 years old she began to have seizures. She was on multiple medications but was still able to build a life. She had a successful business cleaning the homes of "rich" clients in Beverly Hills and was often hired to work parties and dances. She loved her jobs and took care of herself and her three daughters.

But at the age of 38, Flo's seizures became debilitating. Because she was unable to drive, she lost her jobs. Soon she could not afford a place to live, and ended up on the streets. She has been homeless for the past 20 years. When Flo could not get her medications, she turned to drugs. She is now an addict. She says the seizures "make everything worse" because she becomes incapacitated and people steal her belongings. This is how she lost her ID, without which she cannot get services.

Though she enjoys reading and tries to remain positive, falls from her seizures often leave her injured and bruised. She feels that she cannot turn to her family because between her illness and her addiction, she would be "a burden."

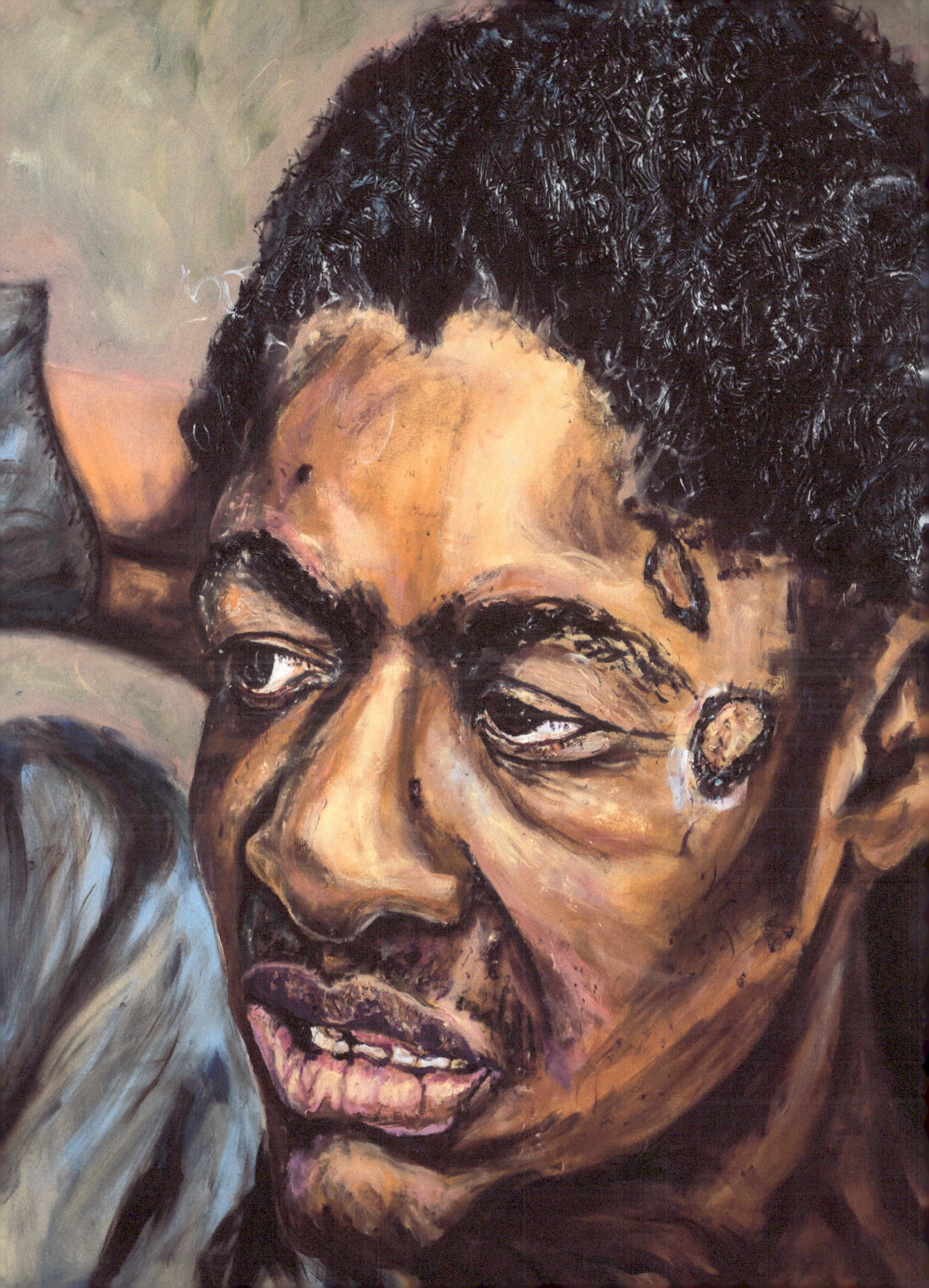

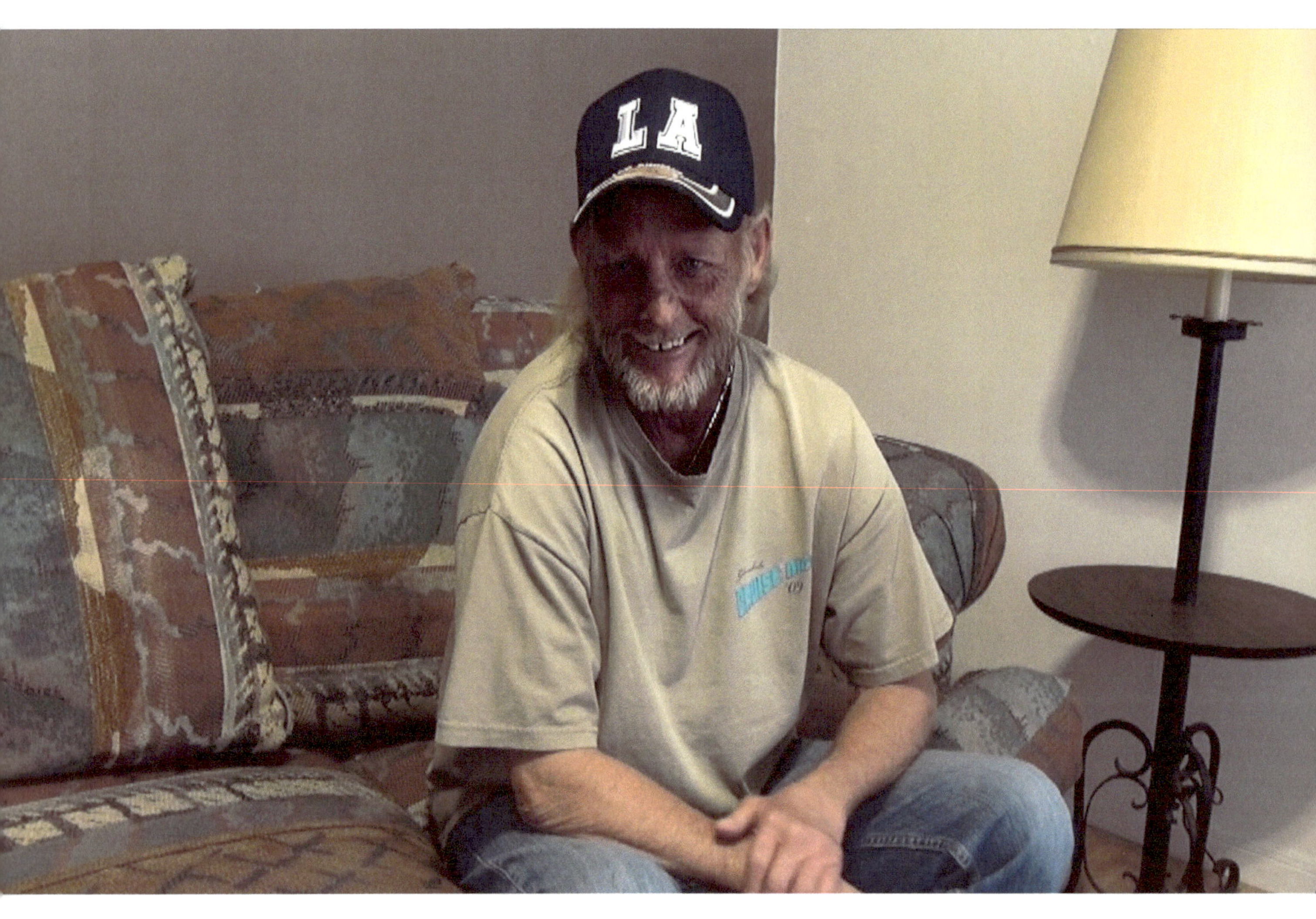

Daniel in his new apartment

Success Stories

I believe most Americans are upset about seeing destitute people living on the streets. They feel overwhelmed by the extent of the problem and don't know what to do about it. Many of us try to help by giving clothes, food, money and smiles, along with understanding and an open heart.

But most of the success stories I have come across in this 10 year journey have been because of dedicated public servants working in government programs. I have worked with many nonprofits and religious organizations who are doing unbelievably wonderful work. Sadly, the scope of the problem has grown to such epidemic proportions that current resources are not sufficient to deal with this issue. We need to build more housing, and we need to come together to welcome our homeless neighbors into our communities and advocate for more supportive services.

One of my greatest joys is when I learn that individuals I have painted are no longer living on the streets, but instead have a roof over their heads. Being homeless limits a person's opportunities to move forward. When survival is the primary goal, there is little time to focus on anything else. But when individuals have a safe place to live, they can then focus on taking care of their physical and mental health, finding employment and becoming productive members of society once again.

Daniel

Daniel's story is one that has haunted me ever since I heard it, because it represents my biggest fear.

An Air Force Intelligence Veteran and a college graduate, Daniel, 50s, worked at AIG Architects in Dallas for 14 years. He began as a draftsman and ultimately became a project coordinator. He had a family, whom he adored.

Then one night, Daniel got a call from the local sheriff informing him that a drunk driver had killed his wife and children.

Daniel "went crazy." He says he "didn't know what [he] was doing." He smoked crack cocaine, slept around, and lost a dangerous amount of weight. Eventually, he came to California and ended up on the beach. Daniel started writing poems, which he calls his "therapy."

After seven years on the beach, Daniel's dream of having his own home came true through the HUD-VASH (Veterans Affairs Supportive Housing) program. He has applied for grants to go back to school and is making plans to start his own car restoration business.

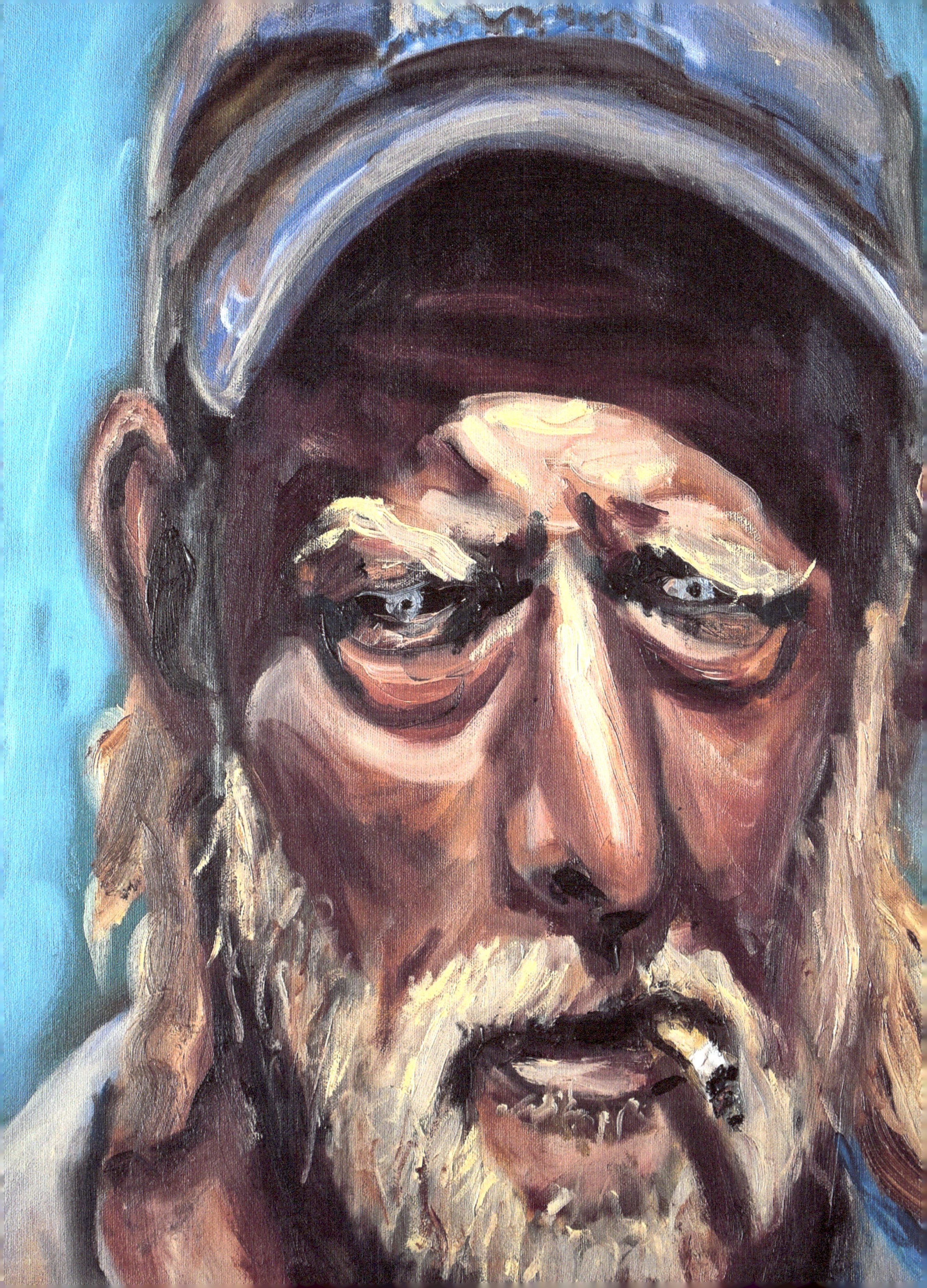

Shamaiah & Children

Abuse from her stepfather was so routine that Shamaiah, 28, assumed this was normal. The Fresh Air Fund program, which sends children from low-income families to upstate New York to live with host families for the summer, showed her how mistaken she was. The knowledge and hope that there was something better for her in the world sustained her back then and "keeps [her] going to this day."

When Shamaiah was eight her parents broke up and she, her mom and her siblings became homeless. Her mom was mentally ill and unable to care for the children. At the age of 20, Shamaiah tried to escape this life by marrying an older man. They had a son. But here too she suffered psychological and verbal abuse. She left and was homeless again. After two years on the streets she became pregnant with her daughter by another man.

To Shamaiah's relief she found shelter in a church. This was the first time in her life she felt cared for. After the birth, Child Protective Services wanted to take her baby away, but the church helped her find services through St. Joseph Center. Shamaiah worked two jobs: one as a receptionist at a spa and another as an administrative assistant. St. Joseph's advocated for her, got her a Section 8 voucher, and found her a "wonderful" apartment where she now lives with her daughter and son.

"Having shelter, a refrigerator, a shower and a bedroom is such a relief…now I can attend to other things. We are starting to put ourselves and our lives back together. We are so grateful and have hope for the future."

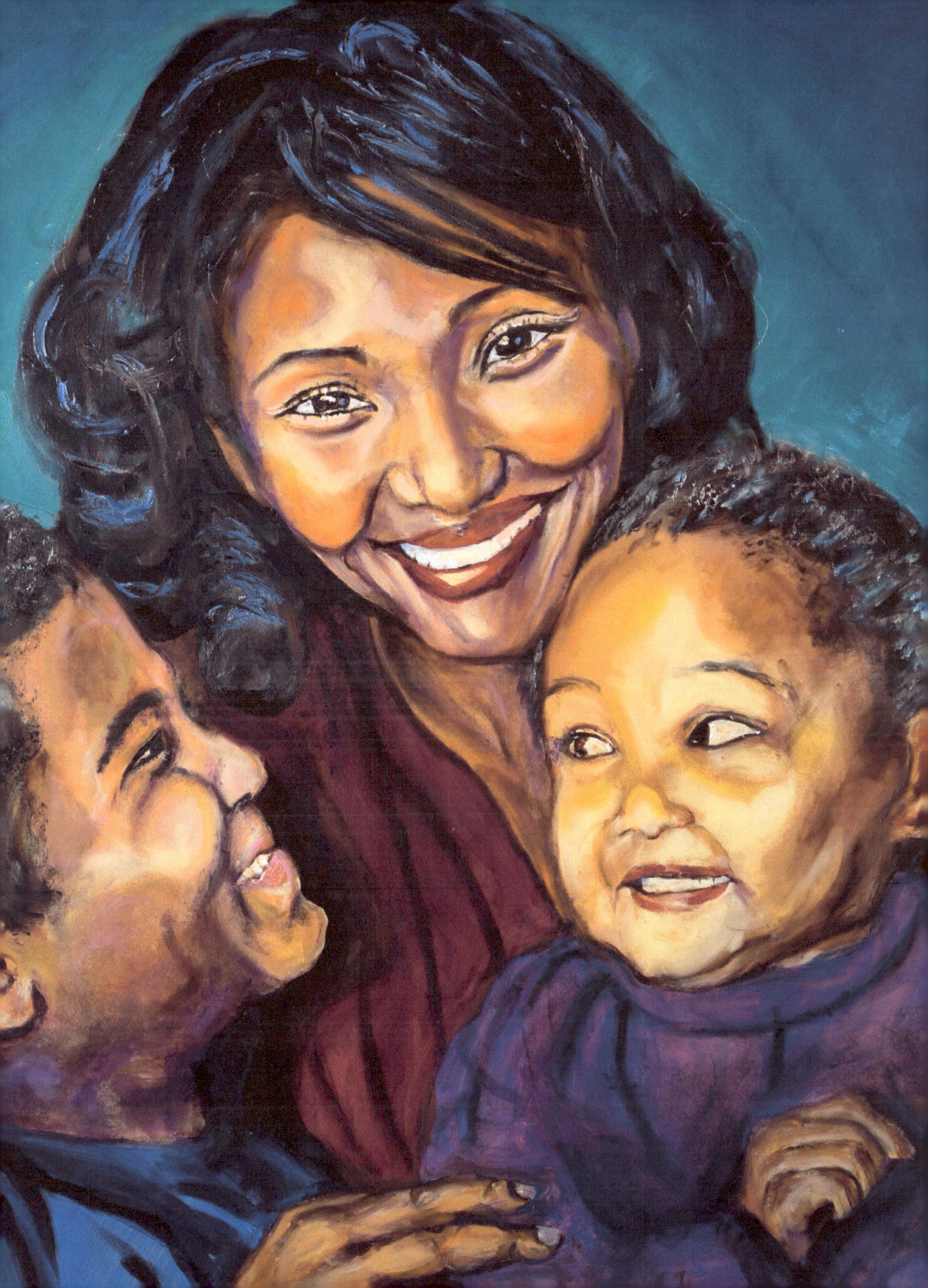

Desiree

Even though Desiree, 20s, is young, she has wisdom far beyond her years. Desiree's mother was a prostitute and drug addict: "We could never invite friends over after school because we would come home to find our mom strung out on crack and speed, thinking there were people in the seams of the mattress." From the age of six Desiree was forced to assume the role of parent – intercepting her mother's food stamps to purchase groceries, so they would not be traded for drugs, and preparing meals for the family.

Desiree struggles to come to terms with her past: "First you think you're fine, then post-traumatic stress sets in and just ruins your world. We realize our mom chose drugs over us, but drugs are so powerful they will make people do that."

Desiree's efforts to find employment have been undermined by unpaid tickets for minor offenses like sleeping in places she was not permitted. Though still homeless, Desiree recently started a job to help former prisoners learn how to cook, and her new employer has agreed to help her clear up the tickets.

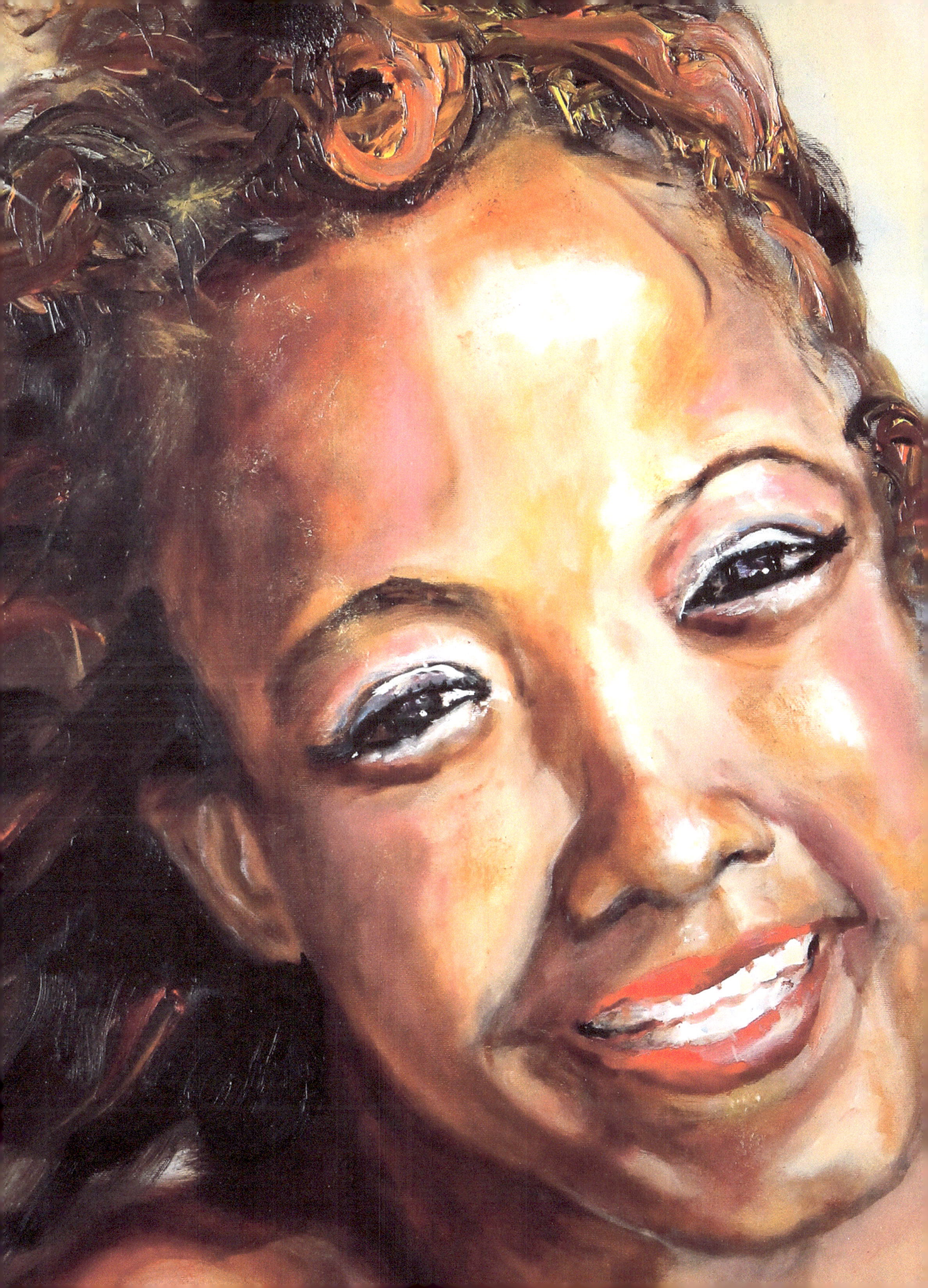

Sunny

Sunny, 62, is one of the sweetest people I have ever met. He was abandoned at birth by his young mother and raised in an orphanage by Catholic nuns. He was a high school football star and an academic standout, accepted to both UC Berkeley and Annapolis. Sunny served in Vietnam and then graduated from Berkeley. He went into business and prospered.

Several years ago, Sunny's wife Jill, also a successful professional, got cancer. He nursed her devotedly, but "slowly, horribly" she died. Having spent everything on her medical bills, Sunny lost their home. Devastated, he began to drink and smoke pot. "Jill fought the battle for two years and lost it, and I've been a piece of s**t ever since ... I can't get over her ... she's still the love of my life."

Sunny tried to get work here but observed that "no one seems to want to hire a homeless person." Not too long ago he relocated to Portland where "they have lots of services." He found work as a dishwasher and cook, and is sober.

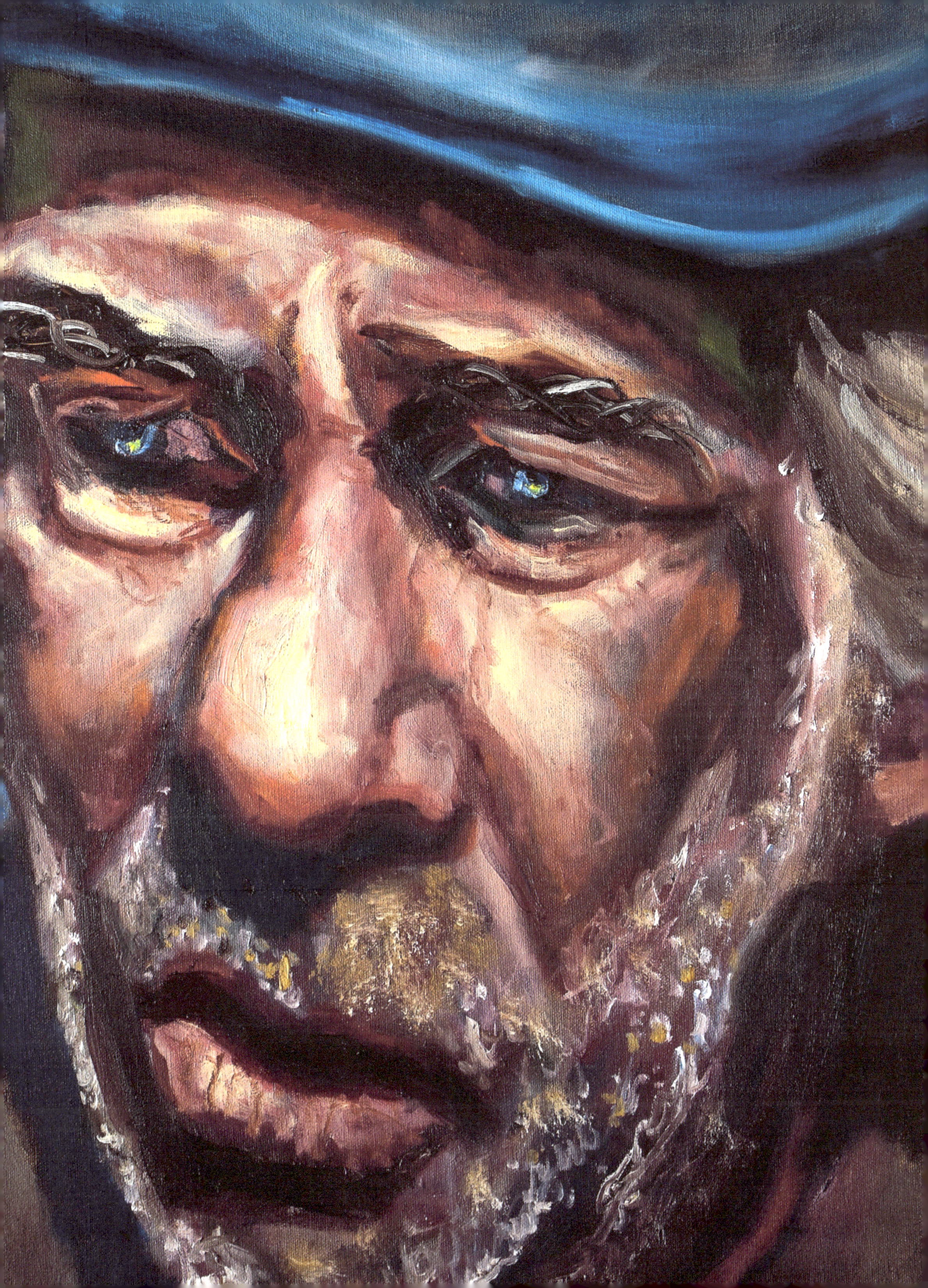

Diane

Diane, 65, walks around wearing a bicycle helmet because she can't stand up straight and keeps falling down. She slurs her words and is constantly off balance. Thirty years ago, she was hit by a car and "everything fell apart." She has a metal plate in her head and suffers from brain damage. She has been homeless since the accident.

Though pregnant at a young age, Diane was able to earn a living, buy a home and support herself and her baby. After the car accident everything changed. She could not raise her son, so her mother took over his care. Diane could not even care for herself.

About 10 years ago, a homeless outreach program was able to get Diane on SSI (Supplemental Security Income) and into a resident hotel on Skid Row. Diane showed me her apartment with great pride. Her room is a cramped, 10' x 10' third floor walkup with just a television, a hot plate and a tiny bathroom. But she is grateful for it every day.

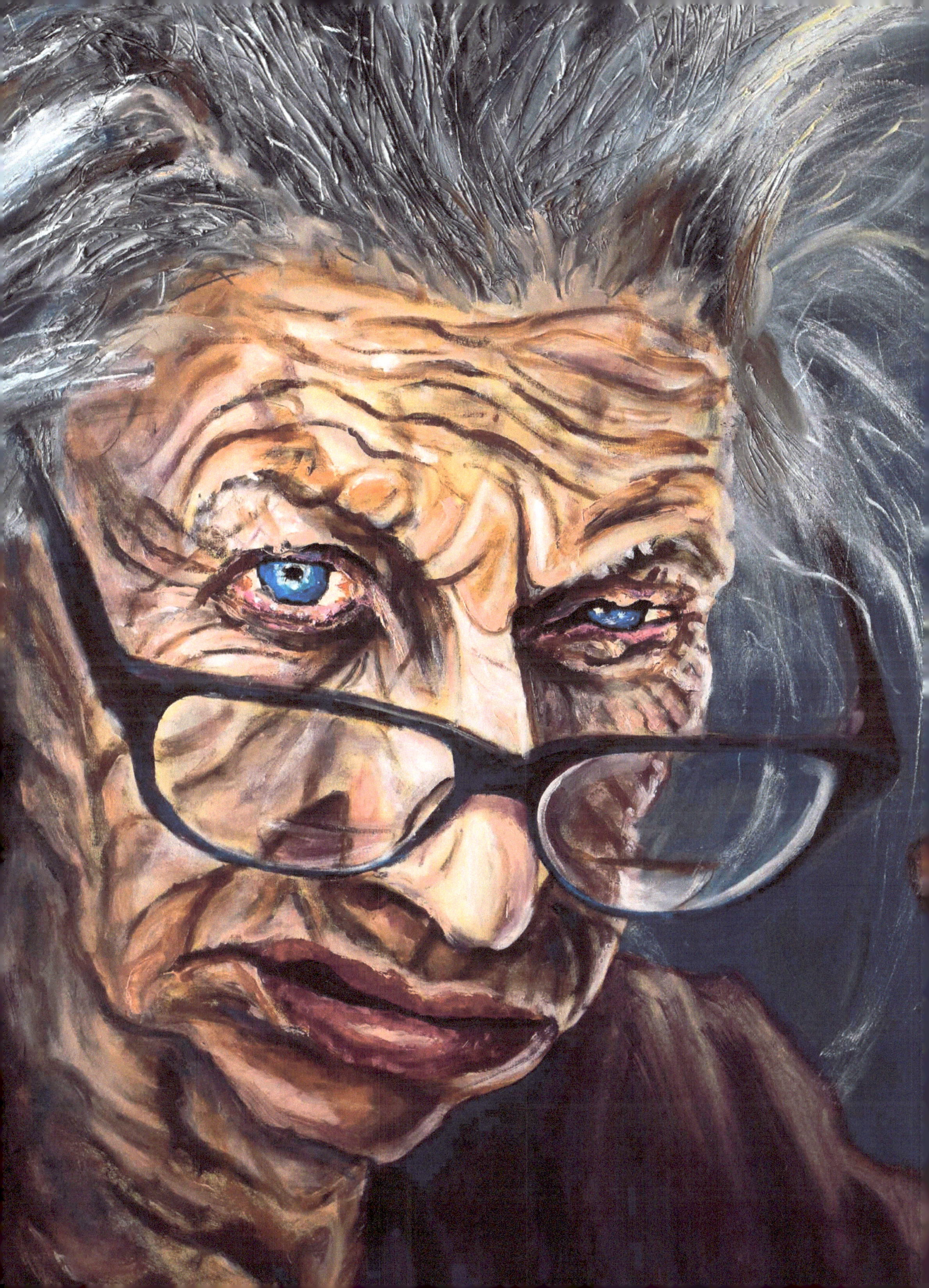

Peggy

When I first went to Skid Row I was frightened. I met Peggy, mid 60s, and she said to stay near her and she would protect me, as she protected a whole group of women. This eased my fear until I got used to going there.

Peggy has led a tragic life. At just nine years old her father, a Command Sergeant in the Army, raped her. When she told her aunt what had happened, Peggy was admonished to stay silent and "get over it." Devastated, Peggy began drinking hard liquor to numb the pain: "I drank half a gallon a day with a straw."

Hoping to escape her demons and make something of herself, Peggy joined the military. But two years into her service she became pregnant and was honorably discharged.

Sadly, her husband of 40 years was physically and emotionally abusive. Peggy finally got the courage to leave and moved in with a friend. But this "friend" drained her savings and stole all her personal belongings. With nowhere else to turn, Peggy ended up on Skid Row. She is now battling throat cancer.

Peggy recently found housing through the HUD voucher program and lives a mile away from Skid Row. She visits often in hopes of helping many of the vulnerable young women she met there get off the streets.

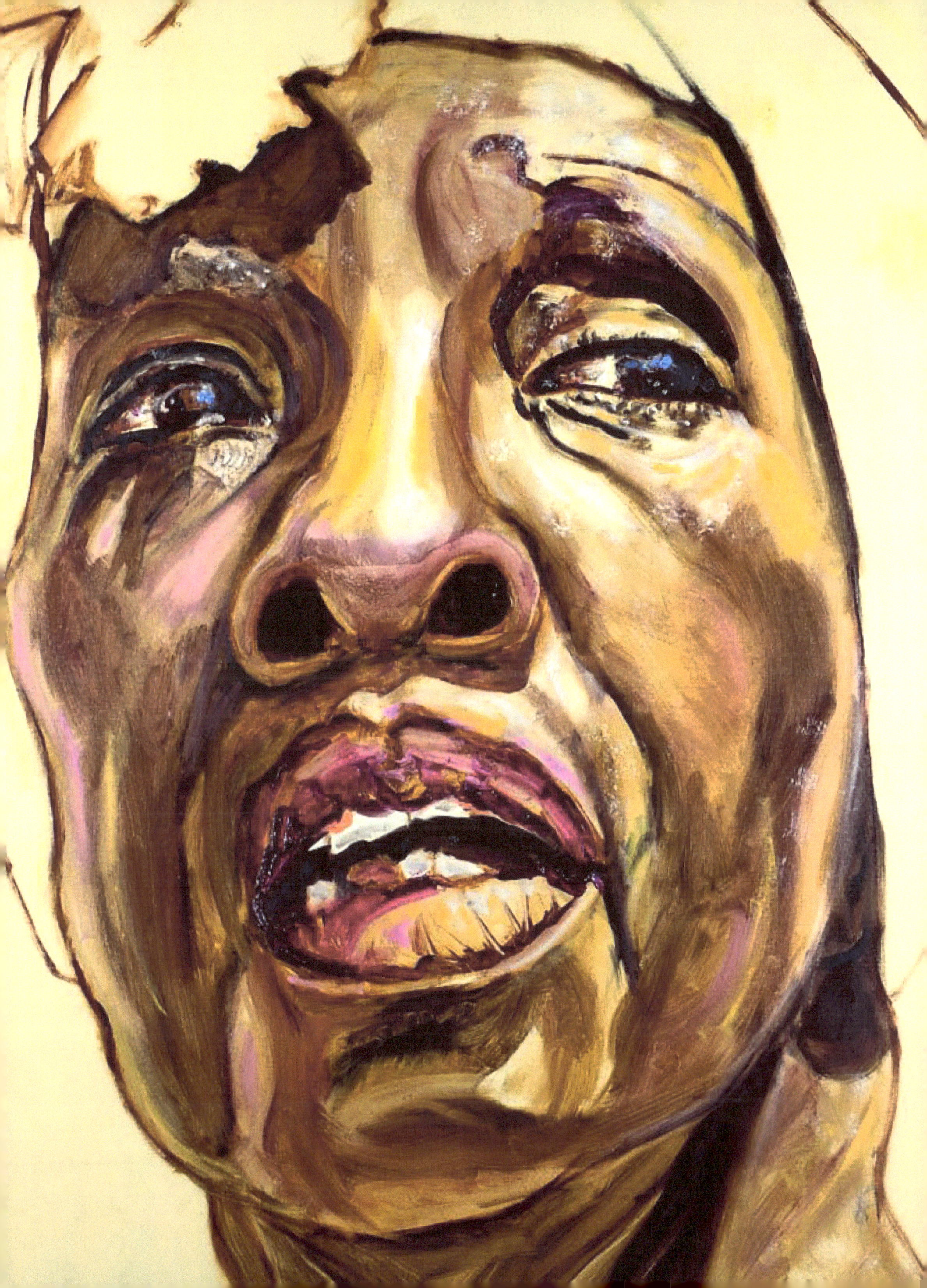

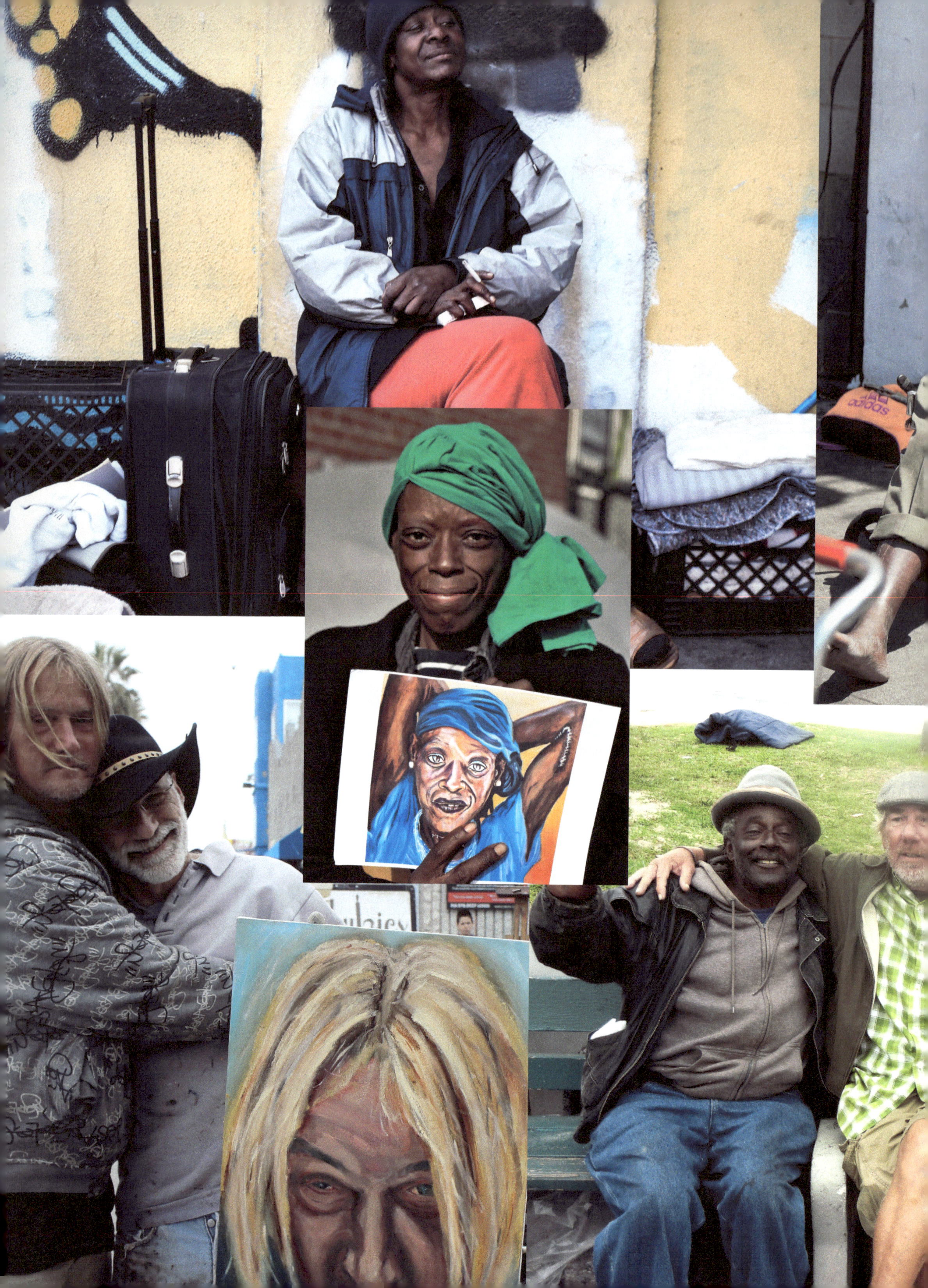

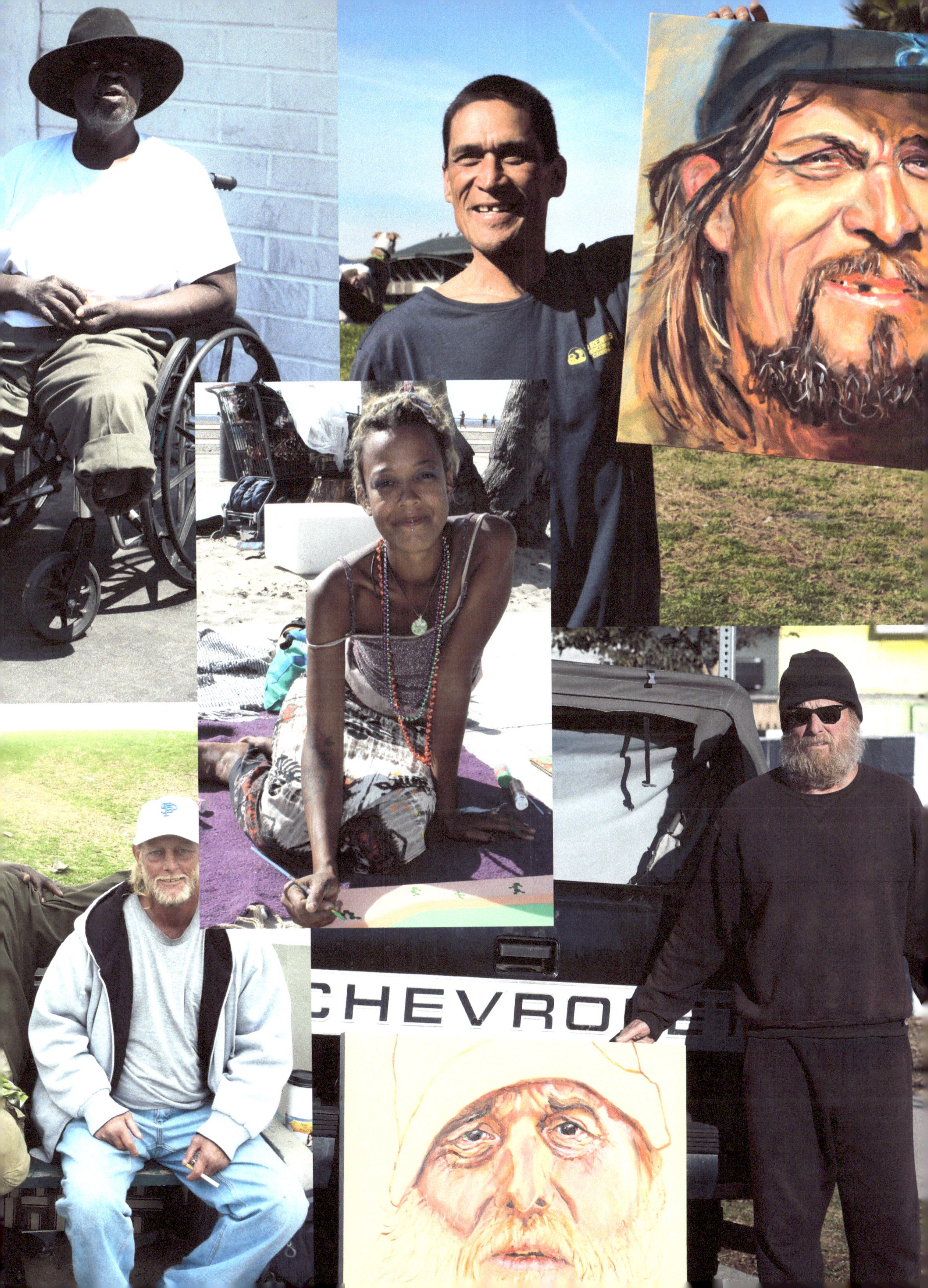

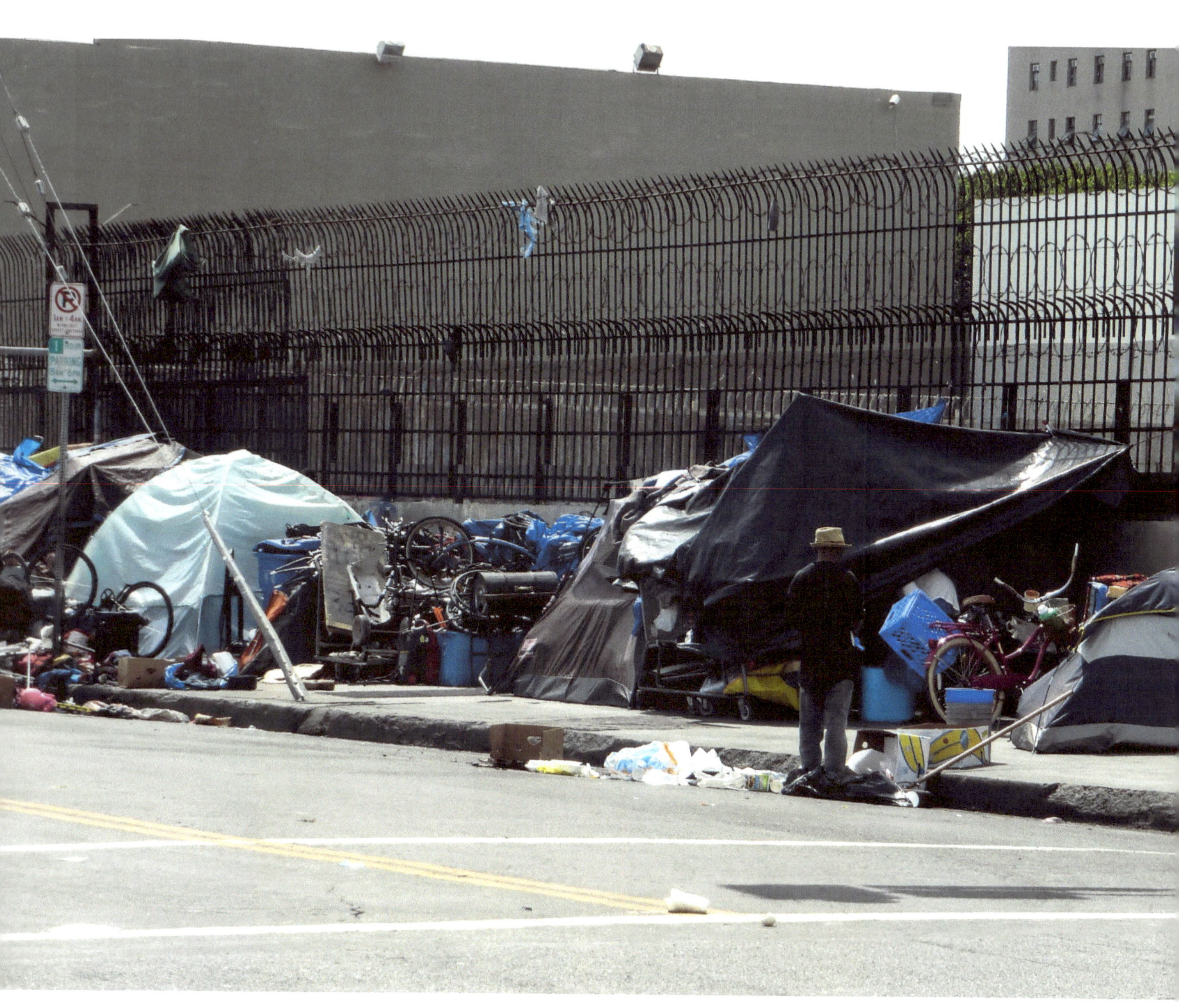

Social Activism

An important fact to consider is that it is about
43% cheaper to house, give services to and help
a homeless person than it is to leave them on the
streets.[1] Individuals experiencing homelessness
often cycle in and out of our medical, mental health
and penal systems, which costs taxpayers money.
Not only does it make financial sense to house our
homeless neighbors, but it makes moral and ethical
sense as well. Mahatma Ghandi said, "A society's
greatness is measured by how it treats its most
vulnerable members."

I believe the choices we are making about people
experiencing homelessness and others in need have
to be rethought. I was told by Los Angeles County
Supervisors that my art exhibitions and activities
have helped humanize this issue in the Los Angeles
public's mind. It is my hope that the stories and
paintings in this book can help shatter stereotypes
about homelessness everywhere. To regard homeless
individuals as the "other," rather than seeing that they
are people just like us, allows a denial of responsibility
and empathy.

[1] *Cousineau, M. and Lander, H.* Homeless Cost Study. United Way
of Greater Los Angeles and Keck School of Medicine (USC);
October, 2009.   *www.homeforgoodLA.org*

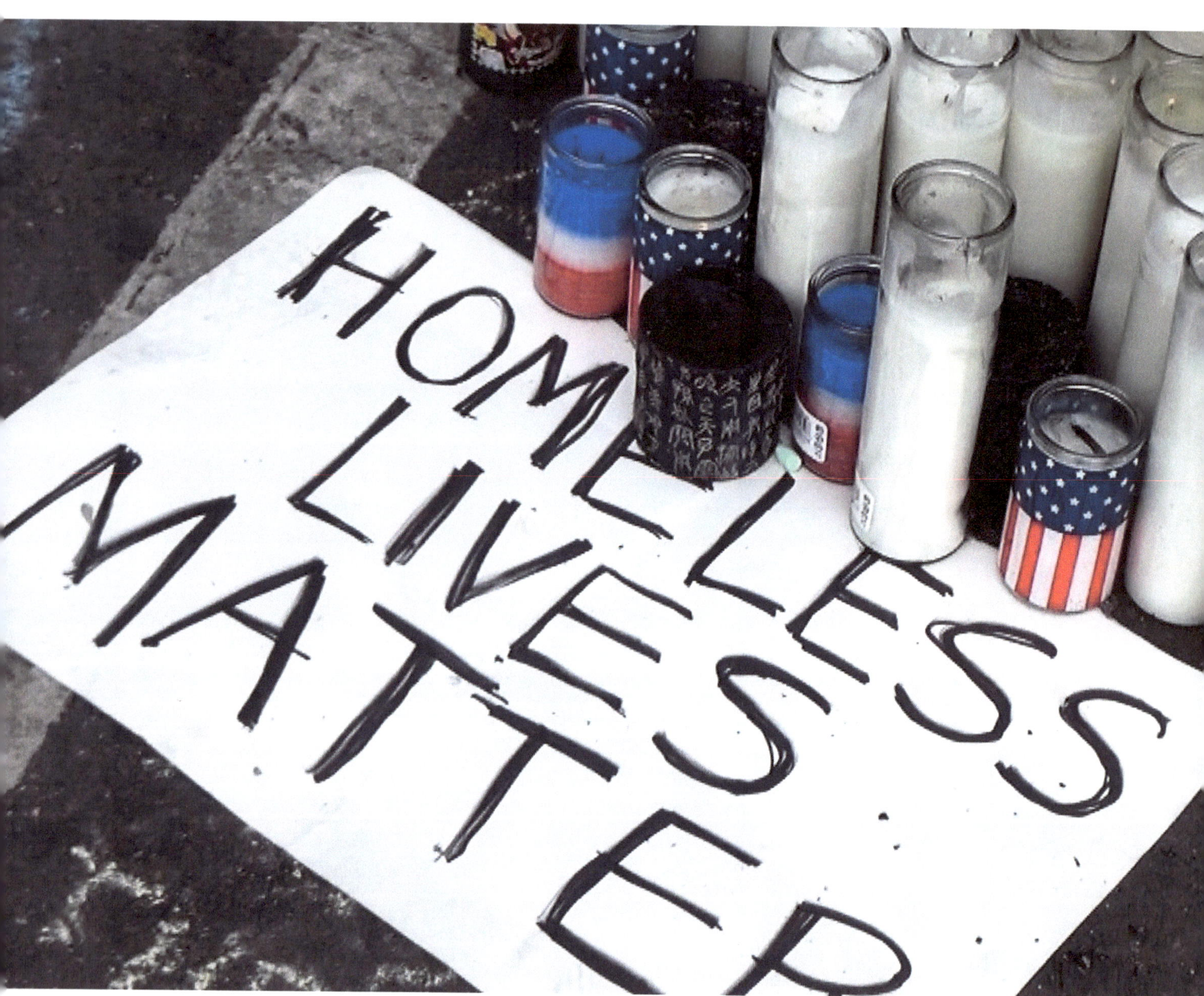

HOMELESS
LIVES
MATTER

What I've Learned

Some simple ideas that I have learned from over 40 years of being a psychotherapist and psychoanalyst that frame this project are:

- All people really want to be loved
- Everyone is trying the best they can
- People are people for good and for bad
- If we can understand a person's circumstances, history and abilities, then where they are and how they got there will become clear
- If someone is in a terrible situation then there is some reason that they are in this predicament and they probably do not want to be there
- Trauma is usually one of the biggest precipitating factors of homelessness

Here is a quote from Barack Obama which expresses part of what I feel:

"The best way to not feel hopeless is to get up and do something. Don't wait for good things to happen to you. If you go out and make some good things happen, you will fill the world with hope, you will fill yourself with hope."

I know that good things have happened for me with this project. I hope that I have also been able to make some good things happen for others.

I believe in small ripples. Small ripples can gain force and make large changes. I started painting people experiencing homelessness to better understand and shine a light on their plight, and to my surprise the project has gained much recognition. There have been exhibitions in movie theatres, houses of worship, corporate and public settings, and in the offices of the Los Angeles Mayor and the L.A. County Board of Supervisors.

Small ripples make a difference.

For more information please visit:
www.stuartperlmanartist.com